GOSPEL FEASTING
104 LORD'S SUPPER DEVOTIONS
FROM THE OLD AND NEW TESTAMENTS

BY MARTIN L. HAWLEY

WILD OLIVE PRESS
APRIL 2015

Gospel Feasting: 104 Lord's Supper Devotions from the Old and New Testaments
Copyright © 2015 by Martin L. Hawley
Woodstock, GA: Wild Olive Press, May 2015

All rights reserved. No part of this publication may be reproduced, distributed, or transmitted in any form or by any means, including photocopying, recording, or other electronic or mechanical methods, without the prior written permission of the author, except in the case of brief quotations embodied in critical reviews, scholarly research, and certain other noncommercial uses permitted by copyright law. For permission requests, contact the author, addressed "Attention: Permissions Coordinator," at the email below:

    wildolivepublishing@gmail.com

ISBN–13: 978-0-9962092-1-2
ISBN–10: 0996209212

Cover and book design by Shari R. Hawley, Wild Olive Press, Woodstock, GA. Author's portrait photograph by Nathan Fowler Photography, Atlanta, GA.

All scripture quotations are from the Holy Bible, English Standard Version® (ESV®), copyright © 2001 by Crossway, a publishing ministry of Good News Publishers. Used by permission. All rights reserved.

Table of Contents

DEDICATION iv

INTRODUCTION v

HOW TO USE THIS BOOK vii

THE RICHNESS OF CHRIST'S GOSPEL FEAST ix

DEVOTIONS FROM THE OLD TESTAMENT 1
    Genesis 3
    Exodus 35
    Leviticus 45
    Numbers 51
    Joshua 53
    Psalms 57
    Isaiah 69
    Jeremiah 79
    Ezekiel 81
    Daniel 85
    Habakkuk 87

DEVOTIONS FROM THE NEW TESTAMENT 89
    Matthew 91
    Mark 99
    Luke 101
    John 109
    Acts 127
    Romans 133
    1 Corinthians 165
    2 Corinthians 171
    Ephesians 173
    Philippians 179
    Hebrews 181
    James 191
    Revelation 193

SCRIPTURE INDEX 213

Dedication

Gospel Feasting is dedicated to the glory of God in Christ Jesus and to all those churchmen who have worked for and who long for the Church's rediscovery of the power of the Lord's Supper as a means of God's grace for His people and as a glorious visual proclamation of the Gospel. Some of these men have been used of God to encourage me specifically along this journey of Gospel Feast rediscovery:

Dr. Sinclair Ferguson
Redeemer Seminary, Dallas, Texas

Dr. Hughes Oliphant Old
Erskine Theological Seminary, Due West, South Carolina

Dr. Robert A. Peterson
Covenant Theological Seminary, St. Louis, Missouri

Dr. Jon Payne
Christ Church Presbyterian, Charleston, South Carolina

Introduction

Why publish a book of Lord's Supper devotions? Why purchase a book of Lord's Supper devotions? These are the typical questions raised by evangelical believers when I tell them about this project — *Gospel Feasting: 104 Lord's Supper devotions from the Old and New Testaments*. The truth is most Protestant Christians and ministers today give little thought to the Lord's Supper as a regular means of God's grace and as an important element in Sunday worship. While a few churches celebrate the Sacrament weekly, most choose to observe it monthly, quarterly, or even less frequently. Further, 21st century pastors are often so preoccupied with the many ministry and administrative tasks they have to perform, that they neglect to prepare their flocks ahead of time for partaking of the Supper. Besides, there are also many schedule pressures on the Sabbath day which make it more convenient for congregations to celebrate Communion infrequently. These same time pressures discourage more focused and more deliberate preparation for the Lord's Supper.

This regrettable neglect of teaching, preparing, and celebrating the Lord's Supper that is so prevalent in our generation has not always been the case in Christ's Church. In fact, roughly between the beginning of the 17th century through the end of the 19th century, or some three hundred years, ministers of the Gospel regularly taught their congregations and helped their members prepare to receive Communion. This teaching and preparation prior to receiving the Lord's Supper was further strengthened by the publication of hundreds of editions of various devotional books, usually small enough to fit inside a coat pocket, and typically referred to as *communicant's manuals*. A quick survey of surviving copies of these volumes reveals that they were written and distributed by Anglicans, Congregationalists, Methodists, and Presbyterians. Typically, they provided some basic instruction on the importance of the Lord's Supper as a means of God's grace, and also presented the communicant reader with a series of devotions that the believer could use prior to Communion as a means of preparing them to receive the bread and the cup.

Sadly, a sharp decline in publication and use of these Lord's Supper manuals set in during the early days of the 20th century. This trend continued unabated throughout the last century, due to a variety of factors which lie outside the scope of this book. However it must be said that there has been a steady decline in emphasis on the Sacrament in much of the Church during the same time period. With less stress placed upon the value of the Lord's Supper, believers saw little reason for taking time to prayerfully prepare to receive it, let alone to go to the trouble of purchasing a book of devotions to guide them in receiving the bread and the cup.

And yet within the past few years, several ministers and Christian authors have begun to address the lack of modern-day communicant's manuals by publishing books with contemporary Lord's Supper devotionals. However, many of these works base the devotions they provide the reader upon popular anecdotes or ministry examples, rather than beginning with the Bible as the foundation and source for their material.

Gospel Feasting represents an effort to publish a 21st century communicant's manual that guides believers in preparing to partake of the Lord's Supper through devotions which are derived entirely from the Word of God. These devotions include both Old and New Testament passages. Why is that? Well, because the Old Testament promises and points the way to Jesus, the person remembered in the Supper, while the New Testament declares Him to be the fulfillment of everything contained in the Old.

Gospel Feasting should only be purchased by Christians who intend to use it regularly. It is a communicant's manual for use in Christ's Church today. It will not be of use to communicants who buy a copy, only to leave it nicely arranged with the other Christian books on their bookshelf. If used often in preparing to receive the Lord's Supper, readers will grow in their knowledge and their faithful appreciation of the Sacrament. They will also deepen their understanding of the unity of the Bible and the great love of God toward all who believe, through Jesus Christ our Savior, the reason for our Gospel Feast.

One final explanation is necessary to the readers of this book, before they begin their journey of preparation for the Supper. *Gospel Feasting* brings back the very out of fashion and yet much more reverent practice of capitalizing the pronouns which refer to God the Father, God the Son, and God the Holy Spirit. The *principle* within each devotion and the example *prayer*, employ this editorial license. It is an additional way in which devotion to the Lord is emphasized using the printed page in this work.

How to Use This Book

BELIEVERS PREPARING FOR THE LORD'S SUPPER

Gospel Feasting is designed for Christians who desire to prepare themselves biblically before coming to the Lord's Table. The work is divided into Old and New Testaments, with devotionals derived from many of the books of the Bible.

The format is extremely simple to follow. Each devotion begins with a selected passage from the Word of God. After the passage, a devotional principle based upon the passage is provided. These are simply labeled for each devotion as principle. The layout for each of the devotions allows each reader to make *Gospel Feasting* their own personal preparation journal for the Supper, adapted to each congregant's particular setting and church community.

Following the devotional principle, each passage includes a written prayer connected with the principle and the Scripture passage. Readers are free to use the prayer, or not use the prayer as they prefer. The prayers are provided as starting points for personal prayer using the Gospel truths illustrated by the Scripture passage within the context of receiving the Lord's Supper. These prayers are set apart in gray boxes at the end of each devotion.

Some readers may wonder at the relative brevity of these devotions and prayers. Many of the earlier communicants manuals of the 17th–19th centuries contain much longer mediations upon Holy Scripture. The main reason for providing these scriptural devotions in a short form is to allow the Supper participant to prepare themselves under the time pressures and busy schedules of the 21st century. These devotions can easily be read, meditated upon, and then prayed within a few minutes, making them convenient for Saturday evening or early Sunday morning use.

PASTORS LOOKING FOR COMMUNION AIDS

This devotional book was also written with working pastors in mind. These Scripture-based devotional principles can be very useful for printing as inserts or within bulletin columns on Communion Sundays. As the devotions are derived from the Bible, they will at times mirror passages that the pastor is preaching on a given Sunday. It is quite effective for the pastor to connect his sermon's Scripture passage to the Lord's Supper, creating a unified worship service for the congregation.

The devotional principles are also useful in providing starting points or summaries for Communion exhortations offered after the sermon. The prayers may assist with formulating Lord's Supper prayers offered by the presiding minister, or may be used in their entirety as desired. The goal is to assist pastors in teaching, preparing, and leading their flocks in rediscovering the beauty, power, and gracious provision of the Lord through the Supper.

Pastors are free to reprint the devotions in this book in their bulletins or inserts without any violation of copyright or royalty fee as long as: 1) They have purchased a copy of the book, and 2) They use the following attribution: *From "Gospel Feasting", copyright © 2015 by Wild Olive Press. Reprinted by permission.* In terms of Sunday school, small group, or other Bible study classes, churches should purchase books for each participant, rather than purchasing one book and photocopying additional copies.

For additional pastoral resources designed to aid in rediscovering the Lord's Supper, a companion volume, *The Gospel Feast: Proclaiming the Gospel Through the Lord's Supper*, is also available. May the Lord our covenant God use this 21st century communicant's manual to draw His people closer to Jesus Christ our Savior, deepen their desire to partake of the Lord's Supper, and increase their hunger and thirst for the amazing grace which the Lord so abundantly provides.

The Richness of Christ's Gospel Feast

The Lord's Supper is one of the means of grace God has given to His Church to sustain and strengthen His people as they walk the wilderness path of faith in this life from salvation to the promise of eternal glory. In combination with Christ-centered proclamation of the Word, prayer, and baptism, the Supper is a vital, essential element in regular biblical worship, preparing the body of Christ as His spotless Bride for the marriage supper of the Lamb. When celebrated according to faith and in the power of the Holy Spirit, the Sacrament is transformative as it ministers to the heart, the mind, and the soul. Ever and always it visually testifies of Jesus Christ crucified and risen from the dead. And with each celebration of Communion, its participants are impacted in different ways, according to the many aspects of the power of God's glorious grace.

At the heart of the Sacrament is *remembrance*, even as Jesus tells His disciples at the Last Supper, *Do this in remembrance of me* (Luke 22:19, 1 Corinthians 11:24–25). The bread serves to remind us of the sinless, guiltless body of Christ, Who bore our sins and our guilt upon Himself when He went as God's suffering servant to die upon that cross as our substitute. And the cup testifies to our redeemed hearts of the new covenant in Jesus blood, which was shed to cleanse us from sin and to purchase our salvation. Every celebration of the Lord's Supper is truly a memorial meal, a gift from God to quicken our awareness of the great price Jesus paid to save us from the dominion of darkness and eternal condemnation. Partaking of the bread and the cup as part of biblical worship is to remember Christ and His saving sacrifice for all who believe in His name.

Connected with remembrance in the Lord's Supper is also *proclamation*. The Apostle Paul revealed in 1 Corinthians 11:26 that, *as often as you eat this bread and drink the cup, you proclaim the Lord's death until he comes*. Thus we can speak of the Supper as *Gospel Feast*. This means, every time we gather together as God's people and participate in the Supper, the Gospel of Jesus Christ is visually proclaimed through the bread and the cup. The Apostle Paul and other New Testament writers describe the Gospel of Jesus Christ as consisting of His saving death, his resurrection and the offer of eternal life. Visual Gospel proclamation is described within the framework provided by God's words of institution from the Gospels or from 1 Corinthians 11:23–26.

This aspect of the Lord's Supper has been forgotten or neglected in much of the modern era, but is slowly being rediscovered and joyfully embraced by the redeemed people of God. As Gospel Feast, the Sacrament serves to preach Christ, both to partaking believers and to those who as yet do not believe, but who are present in the service of worship.

Throughout the history of the Christian Church, the Supper has also been called *Communion*. This is a fitting name for the Sacrament, which is a genuine celebration of the communion which born again children of God enjoy with the Lord and with one another because of the finished work of Christ. As we gather for Communion, we commune by the Holy Spirit with Christ our Savior and also with each other as one body of Christ — a blood-bought family, eternally bound together in the bonds of faith, love, and peace. We who were once cut off from God because of our sin — enemies and strangers to God, in fact — have now been brought near to our Maker and Redeemer thanks to the once-for-all sacrifice of Jesus Christ. And this same sacrifice of Christ has also brought us together with our brothers and sisters in Christ who also believe in His name.

The Lord's Supper may also be described as a *covenant meal*. Much as Moses and the seventy elders of the tribes of Israel were covered with the sprinkled blood, received God's covenant, and then were given the privilege of eating and drinking in the presence of Almighty God (Exodus 24), believers in Jesus come into His spiritual presence covered in His blood as His covenant people and eat the bread and drink the cup. The covenantal aspects of the Lord's Supper are past, present, and future. We celebrate what Christ accomplished on the cross for our salvation in the past. We rejoice in Christ's ministry to us in the present and the outworking of His covenant in our lives. And then we also anticipate the blessed hope of His promised glorious return when all of the blessings of the new covenant will be fully realized in the new heaven and earth. God's great covenants in the Bible reveal not only what God does and how He does it, but also Who God is and why He is worthy of our praise and adoration. As we celebrate Christ's faithfulness to His covenant promises through the Lord's Supper, we truly celebrate the gracious, lovingkindness of God. He keeps His covenant promises faithfully to His chosen people.

As the result of all these aspects of the Supper which the Spirit brings to us when we partake, we can finally also say that the Lord's Table is also truly *Eucharist* — that is, that it is a meal of thanksgiving to God for Jesus Christ, His Son. Every time that we come by faith and celebrate this Gospel Feast, we also give thanks to the Lord for redeeming us eternally from the contamination of our sin and from the holy, just wrath of God. Just as we give thanks to the Lord through prayer and through the singing of psalms, hymns and spiritual songs, so we also give God praise and thanks each and every time that we come to this feast of redemption.

May the Lord our God bring about a rediscovery of the riches of the Lord's Supper in this generation by His Spirit. And may this book of Supper devotions from the Holy Scriptures be one of many instruments in that process. May everyone who reads and uses this book truly find the Lord's Supper to be a *Gospel Feast*.

GOSPEL FEASTING

OLD TESTAMENT LORD'S SUPPER DEVOTIONS

1. The Tree of Life, Jesus Christ, and the Supper

And out of the ground the Lord God made to spring up every tree that is pleasant to the sight and good for food. The tree of life was in the midst of the garden, and the tree of the knowledge of good and evil.

GENESIS 2:9

PRINCIPLE:

God in His goodness provided for His image-bearer Adam every possible good thing, so that there was nothing he lacked in the garden of Eden. According to Genesis 2:9, this included access to eat from the tree of life, which we read in Genesis 3:22 would have enabled Adam to live forever.

Yet there was another tree in Eden. It was the tree of the knowledge of good and evil. Deceived by the serpent, both Adam and Eve disobeyed God's single requirement of them, that they not eat from this particular tree, *for in the day that you eat of it you shall surely die.* Through their disobedience Adam and Eve were separated from fellowship with God and incurred the curse promised them as a result of their sin.

We read at the end of Genesis 3 that the Lord God *drove them out of the garden of Eden to work the ground from which he was taken. He drove out the man, and at the east of the garden of Eden he placed the cherubim and a flaming sword that turned every way to guard the way to the tree of life.* This was actually a merciful act on God's part because had He not done so, man would have remained cursed and separated from God for eternity.

Instead, God in His mercy provided *another* means of access to eternal life — a means of access that not only brings life, but also brings a reversal of the curse. Through Jesus Christ, God's one and only Son, we once again have access to the tree of life, for Jesus is the way, the truth, and the life for all those who truly trust in Him. With the return of Jesus in His glory, the book of Revelation, in chapter 22 promises a restored paradise for redeemed believers in which a river is described flowing from the *throne of God and of the Lamb.* On either side of this river, the Apostle John is shown *the tree of life with its twelve kinds of fruit, yielding its fruit each month.*

As we eat the Lord's Supper together, we are reminded it is only through our Spirit-birthed faith intimacy with Jesus that we may taste eternal life. Jesus is both our *access* to, and in His fullness and blessings, the *essence* of the tree of life. And every covenantal blessing provided to Adam in his original state prior to the Fall is now restored to our inheritance through our redemption in Christ.

> **PRAYER:**
> Gracious and loving heavenly Father, Creator and Sustainer of all things, we thank you that although our first parents Adam and Eve, and we ourselves, sinned against you and were cut off from the tree of life, You restored our access to everlasting life through Jesus, Your Son. We thank you that as Jesus Christ hung on that awful tree He became really and true the new tree of life for all who believe in His name.
>
> As we receive the Lord's Supper, may Your Spirit give us a foretaste of the everlasting life we will one day enjoy in fullness. May the sweetness of born-again life be tasted by faith as we share together in the bread and in the cup. In Jesus' name. Amen.

2. God's Presence and the Supper

> *And they [Adam and Eve] heard the sound of the Lord God walking in the garden in the cool of the day, and the man and his wife hid themselves from the presence of the Lord God among the trees of the garden. But the Lord God called to the man and said to him, "Where are you?"*
>
> Genesis 3:8–9

PRINCIPLE:

Prior to Adam and Eve's disobedience in eating the fruit from the Tree of the Knowledge of Good and Evil, the image-bearers of God enjoyed complete communion with their Creator and experienced His presence in the Garden of Eden. Their sin in violating the single prohibition God gave them to keep brought them both shame and fear. Instead of the wonderful fellowship with the Lord they had previously enjoyed, now they perceived that their communion with God was broken by their willful sin. And yet, the Lord God, fully knowing already what they had done, nevertheless sought them out. In the verses that follow, God deals with the Fall of mankind through Adam by declaring not only the curse, but also His plan to redeem His creation — to *reverse the curse*.

Jesus Christ later came in fulfillment of God's promise as the second Adam. And where the first Adam failed and brought upon all of the creation the great curse, the second Adam obeyed His Father perfectly, died upon the cross, and now is in the process of utterly reversing the curse. As a result of Christ's work, believers in Him are once again granted the astounding privilege of communion with God! This privilege is most evidently displayed and intensified for us as we come together and celebrate the Lord's Supper.

Far from being an empty, symbolic ritual, Communion is celebrated in union with Christ and with our redeemed brothers and sisters according to the faith. This Sacrament reminds us of what Christ did to save us. And yet it also encourages us by the Holy Spirit that Jesus also made us children of God and co-heirs with Him in all the riches of the heavenly places. As a child of the living God, we are invited to dine with the Lord each time that we partake of the bread and cup while gathered for Sabbath worship.

After their fall into sin, when Adam and Eve heard the sound of the Lord walking in the garden and God's voice seeking them out, they hid themselves in fear and in shame. But thanks be to God in Christ that we who believe in Jesus' name no longer have to hide in fear and shame from the Lord. In fact, instead of running away from His presence, we now eagerly seek Him through prayer, through the faithful preaching of His Word, and through the celebration of the Sacraments of baptism and the Lord's Supper, all means of God's glorious and generous grace!

> PRAYER:
> O great Lord God, how amazing it is to me that You, from the very beginning of the creation, have desired intimate fellowship with the men, women, and children you have made in Your image. Father, I am even more astounded and thankful that even though the first Adam sinned against You and brought separation between all mankind and Yourself, You continued to call out to him, saying, "Where are you?"
>
> Through the Covenant of Redemption and the finished work of Jesus Christ Your Son, You also reached out and sought after me. Through the gift of faith You restored communion with me, cleansing my willful sins and my inherited sin, by the blood of Jesus. Gracious and merciful Father, prepare me now to celebrate this restored communion with You around the Table with my adopted brothers and sisters in Christ. Remind me and refresh me through the powerful working of Your Spirit, using these simple elements of bread and the cup. May I always be thankful for the love You poured out for me through the blood of Jesus, represented in the Lord's Supper. Amen.

3. The Heart, Worship, and the Supper

> *In the course of time Cain brought an offering of the fruit of the ground, and Abel also brought of the firstborn of his flock and of their fat portions. And the Lord had regard for Abel and his offering, but for Cain and his offering he had no regard. So Cain was very angry, and his face fell. The Lord said to Cain, "Why are you angry, and why has your face fallen? If you do well, will you not be accepted? And if you do not do well, sin is crouching at the door. Its desire is for you, but you must rule over it."*
>
> GENESIS 4:3–7

PRINCIPLE:

Much theological ink has been spilled trying to describe why it was that Cain's offering was not regarded by the Lord, while Abel's offering was accepted. It is true that Abel's offering resembles the later requirements Yahweh established for sin offerings, something which cannot be said about Cain's offering composed from the fruit of the ground. Animal sacrifice was the means God chose to remind His people that, *the life of the flesh is in the blood, and I have given it for you on the altar to make atonement for your souls* (Leviticus 17:11a). All of the animal sacrifices pointed the way to the once-for-all-time sacrifice of Jesus upon the cross. While the different offerings brought by these first two brothers were no doubt an important element in how their worship was received by God, the more significant difference between Cain and Abel had to do with the condition of their hearts and the rest of their lives, as explained in Hebrews 11:4.

Moses reveals in Genesis 4:5 that when Cain's offering was not regarded by God, his immediate reaction was anger. In fact, the text declares that he wasn't just angry, he was *very* angry. Rather than examine his own heart and life, as well as his offering, Cain was consumed by anger — anger directed against others. We can also discern in the Lord's dialogue with Cain that this firstborn child of Adam and Eve was enslaved by sin. This of course becomes even more evident when we read verses 8–16. Sin's grip upon Cain was such that he murdered his younger brother!

A key principle here for us today is that we cannot *disconnect* the way we worship from the way we live. We cannot easily separate our Lord's Day worship and our celebration of the Lord's Supper from the other six days of our week. While corporate, covenant worship is indeed a time set apart and special, at the same time it is also a culmination and a reflection of the way we have lived before the Lord's face throughout our week. As with Cain, corporate worship reveals the condition of our hearts, the condition of our relationship with the Lord, and the condition of our relationship with one another as members of God's kingdom.

It is important throughout the work week, as we anticipate gathering together for worship, that we submit our hearts and minds to the headship of Jesus Christ and the leading of the Holy Spirit through His Word. We desperately need the help of the Spirit so that sin will not reign over us, and we desperately need the Spirit's work to daily transform our hearts and draw us closer to God and to our brothers and sisters in Christ.

PRAYER:

Heavenly Father, please create in me daily a clean heart, and renew a right spirit within me. Please help me to grow according to Your grace and transforming power working within me. Cause me to see those areas in which I struggle with temptation and fall into sin and sinful patterns. Do your sanctifying work within me daily, preparing me for the day of resurrection glory. Please also do this in me that I may come to worship You and to celebrate the Lord's Supper as a sinner saved by grace, who is being renewed more and more fully, day by day, according to your purposeful, loving plan for my life.

4. Love for Our Brethren and the Supper

And the Lord had regard for Abel and his offering, but for Cain and his offering he had no regard. So Cain was very angry and his face fell.... Cain spoke with Abel his brother. And when they were in the field, Cain rose up against his brother Abel and killed him. Then the Lord said to Cain, "Where is Abel your brother?" He said, "I do not know; am I my brother's keeper?"
Genesis 4:4b–5, 8–9

PRINCIPLE:
As we read the account in Genesis 4 dealing with Cain and Abel and their offerings, we are quickly disturbed to see the depth of hatred the older brother bears for the younger. Perhaps there were many reasons for this animosity. But the way the events are described in this chapter, the immediate cause of the conflict is in Cain's angry reaction to the different ways God engages with them. The Lord looked with favor on Abel and his offering, while Cain and his offering went disregarded by God.

Ultimately we know through the Scriptures that the true root of this conflict was the difference between Cain's heart and Abel's. The Apostle John tells us in 1 John 3:12 that Cain murdered his brother, *because his own deeds were evil and his brother's righteous*. While Abel's heart had been made alive through faith in God and His promise to provide a deliverer from the *seed of the woman*, Cain's heart remained dead and enslaved to sin.

The point John makes in using Cain's murderous behavior as an example is to teach us that *everyone who hates his brother is a murderer, and you know that no murderer has eternal life abiding in him*. And so we should not be surprised that Cain murdered his brother. Cain was *of the evil one*, and without faith was *unable* to love a child of God. John wants believers to clearly understand that we should love one another and that those who have trusted in Jesus by faith and received newness of life are *enabled* to love other Christians. By extension, much like Cain's attack on Abel, we can fully expect those who remain enslaved to sin and the world to hate and to persecute us as well.

The significance of all this for us today in the Church of Jesus Christ is that we are a redeemed family, whose corporate worship (not to mention all of life) should be marked by genuine, Spirit-birthed love for one another. This love for one another should be evident in our services of worship and heightened as we gather around the Lord's Table, which is a meal celebrating our community in Christ. As John later writes, *Beloved, if God so loved us, we also ought to love one another,* (1 John 4:11).

And why was the Apostle Paul so concerned to write about the Lord's Supper to a congregation in 1 Corinthians 11? He was concerned that their heart attitude toward their fellow brothers and sisters in Christ was offensive to God. As they gathered together to receive the Lord's Supper, they treated one another as though they were of the world and dominion of sin, rather than regenerated covenant family by faith in Jesus. In their hearts they were in effect behaving more like Cain, who was of the evil one, than like Abel, who came into God's presence by faith. Through the precious shed blood of Jesus Christ we who believe have been purchased into God's family as His adopted children. We are brothers and sisters one to another. May we display the redeemed condition of our hearts in acts of true love for one another — while gathered for the Lord's Supper and in all and every part of life. In Christ Jesus, we are in fact our brother's keeper!

PRAYER:
Our gracious and loving heavenly Father, thanks to Your mercy and grace shed upon us in Jesus Christ we are part of Your eternal covenant family. We praise, honor, and adore You for causing us to be born again through the gift of saving faith in Jesus. By Your Holy Spirit please deepen our love for You and also for our brothers and sisters in Christ. By the Spirit help us to truly love our neighbor as ourself and to recognize the living local body of Christ gathered for Your Supper. In Jesus' name. Amen.

5. Dwelling in the Tents of the People of God

He [Noah] said, "Cursed be Canaan; a servant of servants shall he be to his brothers. He also said, "Blessed be the Lord, the God of Shem; and let Canaan be his servant. May God enlarge Japheth, and let him dwell in the tents of Shem, and let Canaan be his servant."

GENESIS 9:25–27

PRINCIPLE:
Our presence around the Lord's Table is a regular reminder that it is through the gracious work of Jesus Christ that men and women from every tribe, and language, and people, and nation are admitted into the redeemed people of God (Revelation 5:9–10). The Scripture above from Genesis 9 also serves to remind us that in the early stages of God's dealing with mankind, He chose one people to be called by His name — the descendants of Shem — ultimately the nation of Israel. And yet embedded in this passage is the blessing Noah pronounced upon Shem's brother Japheth, that he would *dwell in the tents of Shem*.

Indeed Shem's descendants, from Abraham to Moses to David to Simeon, who looked with the eyes of faith to God, were marked out and set apart as the Lord's particular people. While the Israelites were supposed to be evangelists for God among the nations, the time had not yet come for large numbers of kingdom conversions, and the tents of Shem (God's people) remained largely inhabited by the families of Abraham.

However, with the arrival of Jesus Christ and His completion of the work of redemption given to Him by His Father, the gates of admission into the chosen people of God were joyfully proclaimed to embrace all the nations — all the descendants of the sons of Noah, who by God's grace were given true faith. With Jesus' ascension into the heavenlies and the outpouring of the powerful Holy Spirit, the trickle of non-Jewish conversions into the people of God became a mighty rushing torrent, spanning the nations of the globe and every generation according to the Lord's redemptive timetable. This ever-growing, ever-flowing stream of converts to faith in Jesus continues to this very hour and will one day cover the earth as the waters cover the sea. The rising tide of God's redeeming love will finally crescendo with the glorious final appearing of Christ.

Through the sin-bearing body and cleansing blood of Christ, all those who call upon the name of the Lord in Him will be saved. And through the name of Jesus we are all made one people for God, a kingdom of priests to ever serve in His kingdom. The fellowship we share around the table of the Lord's Supper signifies for us the unity and the common kingdom 'nationality' we share in Christ our Lord. How fitting it was for Noah to prophetically bless the sons of Japheth by declaring God's manifold grace to them. And the fulfillment of this "dwelling in the tents of Shem" is for us to share in the identity of God's chosen people and the hospitality of His glorious kingdom!

PRAYER:
Heavenly Father, we thank you that although we were not Your people according to the bloodline of Abraham, You have chosen to make us part of Your people through the shed blood of Jesus, Your Son. Indeed we are the wild olive branches which you have grafted into your cultivated tree. May we have opened eyes to see and redeemed minds to understand the wideness and diversity of the family of God among whom you have made us a part. May we rejoice together with brothers and sisters from every sort of nation, language, culture, and economic circumstances, knowing that we are one holy nation, a kingdom of priests, purchased by the one and the same blood of Christ. In Jesus' name we pray. Amen.

6. The Covenant and the Supper

> *Now the Lord said to Abram, "Go from your country and your kindred and your father's house to the land that I will show you. And I will make of you a great nation, and I will bless you and make your name great, so that you will be a blessing. I will bless those who bless you, and him who dishonors you I will curse, and in you all the families of the earth shall be blessed."*
>
> GENESIS 12:1–3

PRINCIPLE:

The God of the universe is also the God of the covenant. The Lord enters into relationship with His people by means of covenants, just as we read in God's dealings with Abram (Abraham). Yahweh, the living God, always initiates the covenants He makes. In Abraham's case, the Lord requires him to leave behind all that he has ever known in exchange for a promised land that he knows nothing about. As part of God's covenant, He makes certain promises of blessing to those who are faithful to Him. The promises of God to Abraham included; making of him a great nation, a divine blessing, a great name, a curse on his enemies, and a blessing for all the families of the earth through him.

When God chose to formalize His relationship with Abraham through a covenant ceremony (see Genesis 15:5–6), we read that, *he believed the Lord, and he counted it to him as righteousness.* Abraham's relationship with Yahweh was not based upon anything Abraham had done, or anything special about his person. His covenant bond with God was based upon God's choosing and through the living faith Abraham exercised toward his God.

The promises God made to Abraham, which he trusted in through the gift of faith, were ultimately fulfilled in the person and work of Jesus Christ. As Jesus fulfilled the Abrahamic Covenant, He also fulfilled what we understand to be the Covenant of Redemption, which God the Father and God the Son entered into before the Fall and even before the world was made. In fulfilling all of the covenantal promises of Yahweh, Jesus indeed blessed *all of the families of the earth* through the gift of salvation to all who truly believe in Him.

When Jesus told the disciples on the night He was betrayed that the cup of blessing *that is poured out for you is the new covenant in my blood* (Luke 22:20), He was announcing to them that the Covenant of Redemption and the Abrahamic Covenant were about to be fulfilled through His shed blood upon the cross. The command of Jesus to the Apostle Paul, *Do this, as often as you drink it, in remembrance of me* (1 Corinthians 11:25), teaches us that as followers of Christ, we are to gather as the covenant people of God to remember, and to celebrate the realization of the covenant promises through Jesus Christ.

> PRAYER:
>
> Thank you heavenly Father, that You desire to have fellowship with me and all those You call Your people by means of covenants. Praise and honor and glory and blessing to You and to Your Son for together providing for my redemption from sin before the world existed! Lord Jesus Christ, thank You for your atoning sacrifice, whose blood sealed my salvation and brings me the precious and priceless blessings of the covenant! Thank You Holy Spirit, for enabling me to see with the eyes of faith, as did my father Abraham, the reality and certainty of God's promises! And thank You, wonderful Spirit, for applying to me the benefits and blessings which flow from Jesus Christ! Help me now to see with the eyes of faith, the fulfillment of the covenants and promises of God through Christ, in the visible symbols set before me in the Lord's Supper. Amen.

7. Melchizedek and the Supper

After his return from the defeat of Chedorlaomer and the kings who were with him, the king of Sodom went out to meet him at the Valley of Shaveh (that is, the King's Valley). And Melchizedek king of Salem brought out bread and wine. (He was priest of God Most High.) And he blessed him and said,
> *"Blessed be Abram by God Most High,*
> *Possessor of heaven and earth;*
> *and blessed be God Most High,*
> *who has delivered your enemies into your hand!"*
And Abram gave him a tenth of everything.

GENESIS 14:17–20

PRINCIPLE:
Many of the greatest theologians throughout history have attempted to identify all of the *types* or *shadows* of Jesus Christ located within the Old Testament Scriptures. Clearly, God chose in various ways to prepare His people for the coming of His Son through the incarnation. He did this by means of persons and ceremonies that would depict Jesus' future offices and work.

In the case of Melchizedek, this mysterious kingly and priestly figure, there is no doubt that a type or shadow is intended for Christ. Some argue that Melchizedek is in fact an Old Testament *Christophany*, a pre-incarnate appearance of Christ Himself! We know that God intends us to learn from Melchizedek something about Christ because it is clearly revealed for us in the Epistle to the Hebrews, chapter 7:

For this Melchizedek, king of Salem, priest of the Most High God, met Abraham returning from the slaughter of the kings and blessed him, and to him Abraham apportioned a tenth of everything. He is first, by translation of his name, king of righteousness, and then he is also king of Salem, that is, king of peace. He is without father or mother or genealogy, having neither beginning of days nor end of life, but resembling the Son of God he continues a priest forever.

It is then to this king of righteousness and peace — to this priest of God Most High — that Abram, the man of faith, comes and receives both bread and wine, and particularly divine blessing. One cannot help but see this important event in Abram's life as a time of worship of and communion with God, through the priestly ministry of Melchizedek.

And so it is when we come seeking to worship the Most High God, that we do so through the ministry of Jesus Christ, King of righteousness and peace, the great High Priest, who always lives to intercede for us. Communion with God Most High is mediated to us by the Spirit of God through the work of Christ and represented to us by bread and wine. Through our faithful participation in worship and communion at the Lord's Table, we receive divine blessing and grace.

PRAYER:

Heavenly Father, God of Abraham, Isaac, and Jacob, and my God, thank you for providing a great High Priest in your service, to make propitiation for my sins. I am completely unworthy and undeserving of Your grace and mercy shown to me through Jesus Christ, Your Son, who comes not in the likeness of Aaron and the Mosaic priesthood, but in the likeness of Melchizedek, king of righteousness and peace, Your perfect priest. Thank You that Jesus my Savior is the guarantor of a better covenant who saves me to the uttermost! Thank You for the bread and the wine which provide spiritual grace and divine blessing, pointing us to our great High Priest and bringing to our hearts and minds the benefits of His pierced body and shed blood. Indeed, blessed are You, God Most High, who through Christ, have delivered us from our enemies, sin, death, hell, and Satan. Amen.

8. The God Who Sees Me and the Supper

So she called the name of the Lord who spoke to her, "You are a God of seeing," for she said, "truly here I have seen him who looks after me." Therefore the well is called Beer-lahai-roi (the well of the Living One who sees me); it lies between Kadesh and Bered.

GENESIS 16:13–14

PRINCIPLE:
In the story of Hagar's encounter with the Angel of the Lord, we find comforting revelation concerning the character of God. Hagar was a female Egyptian servant who was part of Abram's household. Abram's barren wife, Sarai, contrived to obtain children through Hagar, and permitted her husband to take her as a wife. Hagar did conceive as a result of this scheme. However, there began to be strife between Sarai and Hagar. After receiving harsh treatment, Hagar fled from Sarai into the wilderness. It was there that the Angel of the Lord appeared to her with words of comfort, provision, and hope.

The Lord told Hagar that He had heard the cries of her affliction, and he promised her that He would multiply her offspring *so that they cannot be numbered for multitude*. During her encounter with the Angel of the Lord, Hagar learned that God indeed hears the cries of those in distress and that He sees their afflictions. The name given her son, Ishmael, conveys this great truth about God, for the name means simply, *God hears*. In His compassion and mercy God does indeed *look after* the outcast and downtrodden.

It is encouraging that God would so such concern for Hagar and her unborn child. After all, Hagar's child was not to be the designated heir to the covenant promises, and was conceived not according to God's *revealed* will, but according to the doubts and scheme of Sarai and Abram. Hagar had also shown contempt towards her rightful mistress and the woman through which the promised covenant heir would one day come.

We indeed glimpse in the Lord's general lovingkindness and provision for Hagar and her unborn child something of the particular lovingkindness and provision He has so freely extended to us who are redeemed in Jesus His Son. As Gentiles, we were once alienated from the promises of God, lost and alone in the wilderness of sin, despair, and eternal condemnation. And yet all along El-Roi, the God who sees, purposed to provide for our salvation, our hope, and our eternal justification through the gift of faith in the work of Jesus Christ. Along with this amazing provision from the hand of God, we also draw daily comfort from the great truth that the Lord continually sees and continually hears the prayers of those who call upon him in faith. His provision is abundant and constant, and His all-seeing presence abides with us always.

As we come to the Lord's Table, let us reflect prayerfully on the lovingkindness and gracious provision of God for us through the body and blood of Jesus Christ. God our Father understood our need in eternity past and He covenanted with His Son to redeem us. He clearly saw the desperation and hopelessness of our need, and He provided abundantly with the one and only means by which we could be delivered from eternity separated from Him. By faith in Jesus, our tortured cries of affliction have become joyful cries of redemption!

PRAYER:

Heavenly Father, we thank you today for Your abundant compassion for us, compassion which led to decisive action. You did not leave us in hopelessness and despair. You did not abandon us to an eternity in torment because of our sins. But instead you delivered us from our helpless estate by providing a substitute — the Lord Jesus Christ. Thank you for providing for all of our needs in this life and the life which is to come through the work of Christ and through the indwelling of the Holy Spirit. Please enable us and move us to exuberant thankfulness as we partake of the bounty of Your Table and its symbols of Your lavish and costly love for us. In Jesus' name. Amen.

9. The Promise and the Fulfillment of a Son and the Supper

And God said to Abraham, "As for Sarai your wife, you shall not call her name Sarai, but Sarah shall be her name. I will bless her, and moreover, I will give you a son by her. I will bless her, and she shall become nations; kings of peoples shall come from her."

GENESIS 17:15–16

PRINCIPLE:
The Lord is a covenant-keeping God. That means that when He makes a promise to provide for His people, He will ever and always deliver on that promise. An early example of God's faithfulness in Scripture is the promise He made to Abraham to provide for him a true son and heir. Abraham had every reason to doubt God's promise based upon the outward appearance of things. He was quite old and his wife Sarah was well beyond the age for bearing children. They had been married for decades and there had never been a child. Perhaps we can understand somewhat how Abraham and Sarah took matters into their own hands and used Hagar to conceive a child.

But God was faithful to fulfill His promise to give Abraham and Sarah a son. The Lord's promise was fulfilled with the birth of Isaac, precisely as the Lord had declared. This faithful consistency — this lovingkindness to provide for His people — is displayed even more beautifully in the promise God made to provide a son, the Son — His Son — to redeem the world. In the prophecy of Isaiah 7:14 we read:

Therefore the Lord himself will give you a sign. Behold the virgin shall conceive and bear a son, and shall call his name Immanuel.

This promise was fulfilled for God's people when in the course of time and according to the Lord's predetermined plan, the Lord Jesus Christ was born to a young virgin named Mary in Bethlehem some 2,000 years ago. Jesus was the greatest Son of the promise, because in Him, every promise to the adopted children of God was confirmed and sealed. And we celebrate that even the name given to him by the prophet some 600 to 700 years before His birth was fulfilled. For this promised Son who came and dwelt among us was indeed really and truly *God with us*!

And so as we gather around the Lord's Table we celebrate that the Lord's promise to His people — to us who believe by faith — was fulfilled in the incarnation and birth of Jesus Christ. And through His life, death, resurrection, and ascension we continue to enjoy His presence. For by the work of God's Holy Spirit, the Son remains Immanuel, the God who is with us. May the Spirit of Christ remind us at the Supper today that Jesus is ever with us, *even unto the end of the age.*

PRAYER:

Heavenly Father, we thank You that you fulfilled Your promise to Abraham and Sarah, giving them the son of promise, Isaac. We thank You that Isaac was part of Your redemptive plan through the descendants of Abraham to one day bring Your own Son of promise Jesus Christ into this world. We thank You that the Lord Jesus came at the proper time and identified with us, that He lived a sinless life, and that He suffered and He died in our place, bearing our sins away upon the cross on Calvary. We praise You and thank You for Your faithfulness and for keeping Your covenant promise of redemption. We also praise Jesus Your Son for taking the form of a servant and enduring so very, very much in order to save us from our sins and our sins' consequences. In Jesus' name we pray. Amen.

10. The Mercy of a Just God and the Supper

So the men turned from there and went toward Sodom, but Abraham still stood before the Lord. Then Abraham drew near and said, "Will you indeed sweep away the righteous with the wicked?... Far be that from you! Shall not the Judge of all the earth do what is just?" And the Lord said, "If I find at Sodom fifty righteous in the city, I will spare the whole place for their sake."

Genesis 18:22–23, 25b–26

PRINCIPLE:
The Patriarch Abraham understood something of the character of God when he interceded with the Lord for the people of Sodom. Abraham knew the Lord to be utterly holy and entirely just in His execution of judgment upon the wicked. He also knew that God was ever and always faithful to carry out His revealed intentions and that Yahweh would do precisely to Sodom and Gomorrah what He had revealed to Abraham.

Now we might also believe that the Patriarch of the Faith interceded before God for the lives of those in Sodom based entirely upon this same divine characteristic of utter justness. Yet the key to Abraham's boldness and persistence in pleading with the Lord was his understanding of the mercy of God toward His covenant people. In the truest sense of the word, no one in Sodom was *righteous*, not even Lot himself — at least in the way of inherent personal righteousness. Those Abraham identified as righteous were just so because they belonged to God. They believed in Him, and as with Abraham were reckoned as righteous based upon faith. Abraham was therefore asking, not that the Lord save them for anything that they had done, but rather that they receive God's mercy because they belonged to Him.

Ultimately, we know that God in fact judged Sodom and Gomorrah with fierce fire and brimstone (Genesis 19:23–29). Yet the Lord did hear and regard Abraham's prayer in the sense that those who belonged to the Lord — Lot and his family — were delivered from the city before it was destroyed. The Scriptures identify Lot as righteous, and apparently he was also an heir of the covenant through his connection with Abraham.

While there are differences in the circumstances, each of us who believe in Jesus Christ are accounted as righteous in God's sight through our Savior's completed work. As such, we receive the greatest of mercy from the Judge of judges. We are delivered from the eternal destruction of fire and brimstone that awaits the unsaved on the day of the Lord's return. We continue in this life, in fact, even in the midst of a wicked and perverse culture, purely due to the mercies of God our Father in Christ His Son.

When we come to the Lord's Supper, His Spirit reminds us of the mercies of God in Christ, Who bore the wrath of God's judgment against our sin and made us to be righteous heirs of His gracious covenant. By His shed blood and sin-bearing body, we have been spared the destruction which awaits those who reject God's Lordship. And it is through His daily common mercy and forebearance that we and those around us — regenerate and unregenerate — continue to enjoy this life we have been given in the here and now.

> **PRAYER:**
> Our gracious heavenly Father, we honor You and we adore You for Who You are and for all Your mighty works. Thank You for providing the way of escape for us from the certainty of eternal damnation in the fires of hell. Thank You for declaring us to be righteous — not because of any holiness that we possess but because Your sinless, holy Son Jesus Christ has died for us. Thank You that in Jesus by faith we are justified — declared righteous in Your sight. In Jesus' holy name. Amen.

11. The Beloved Son's Offering, the Substitute, and the Supper

After these things God tested Abraham and said to him, "Abraham!" And he said, "Here am I." He said, "Take your son, your only son Isaac, whom you love, and go to the land of Moriah, and offer him there as a burnt offering on one of the mountains of which I shall tell you."

GENESIS 22:1–2

PRINCIPLE:

Abraham's obedient willingness to offer his cherished son as a sacrifice to Yahweh is one of the most important events in God's unfolding redemptive plan. While some Bible teachers choose to emphasize Abraham's faith and obedience revealed in the details of the story, others point out the event's parallels with God the Father's willingness to offer His one and only Son to be our substitute, to make atonement for our sins. In fact, the Hebrew used in verse 2, rendered *your only son..., whom you love*, echoes the language used to describe God's own Son.

And yet, while these are crucial elements in understanding this important historical event, perhaps the most significant is the truth that just before the death of Isaac could take place, the Lord God provided a substitute for the sacrifice — *a ram, caught in a thicket by his horns* (Genesis 22:13). What a test this whole turn of events was for His servant, Abraham! After all, this was the patriarch's son, his *only son, whom he loved*, a description later used to describe God's relationship with His only Son, Jesus. What a joyous relief it must have been for this devoted father to see Isaac, the son of God's promise, spared from death by his own father's hands.

Ultimately, because of sin, all of us deserve to be put into the position that Abraham was asked to place Isaac into, dying to pay the penalty rightly due to God. However, as with Isaac, God in His great lovingkindness and mercy, reveals Himself to us as *The Lord will provide*, and places His Son, His only Son upon the cross to die in our place. It is God's gracious and glorious exchange of Christ for us. As the Scripture declares, *All we like sheep have gone astray; we have turned — every one — to his own way; and the Lord has laid on him the iniquity of us all* (Isaiah 53:6). Redemptively speaking, Christ is foreshadowed, or represented, in both Isaac and in the substitutionary ram! This substitution God has made for us through His one and only Son is recounted every time we celebrate the Lord's Supper. When we are able to see this great eternal truth through the eyes of faith as we come to the Lord's Table, our experience of the Sacrament is so much more than a familiar ritual or repetitive religious rite.

PRAYER:
Faithful Lord and Provider, thank You that You have provided a substitute for me — someone to bear the stains and penalties for my awful sins — Jesus Christ, Your one and only precious Son, whom You chose to hang in my place. Thank You, Lord Jesus Christ, spotless Lamb of God, my *ram caught in a thicket*, that You were willing and committed to suffer and die so that I might live!

Thank You, Father, Son, and Holy Spirit, for reminding me, each time You call me to Your Table, of these astounding and transforming truths. Show me with each Communion celebration a glimpse of the Your glory in Christ, and work within me a deeper understanding of the price Jesus paid and the separation borne while hanging upon that cross. Amen.

12. Not Because of Our Works or Our Wily Scheming

So Jacob went near to Isaac his father, who felt him and said, "The voice is Jacob's voice, but the hands are the hands of Esau." And he did not recognize him, because his hands were hairy like his brother Esau's hands. So he blessed him. He said, "Are you really my son Esau?" He answered, "I am." Then he said, "Bring it near to me, that I may eat of my son's game and bless you." So he brought it near to him, and he ate; and he brought him wine, and he drank.

GENESIS 27:22–25

PRINCIPLE:

The character and life of the patriarch Jacob continually paint for us a portrait of someone who persists in believing that in order to receive God's promised blessing, you must be resourceful and cunning. It was not enough for Jacob to have God speak directly to him and assure him that His blessing to Abraham and to his father Isaac would now rest upon him. It was not enough for Jacob that God had revealed to his mother that his older brother Esau would one day serve him. Instead, Jacob always sought to obtain the promises of God's blessing by trickery, skill, and outright deceit. Jacob was willing to take advantage of his brother in order to obtain the birthright (Genesis 25:30–34), and now at the end of his father's life, with Isaac's eyes gone very dim, Jacob proceeds to lie to his aged father, in order to take away Esau's blessing.

So what do we take away for our own life and faith from the account of God's dealings with Jacob? Well, besides our amazement at the patience and grace of God, we must see that the overarching lesson is the electing power of God, choosing the recipients of His Covenant of Redemption purely according to His own purposes. Jacob did not have to resort to these sinful, man-centered methods in order to obtain what God had already promised to him. In fact, by seeking to obtain the blessings and provision of God by deceit, Jacob wrecked his relationship with his brother, and even with his likewise deceitful uncle, Laban. And yet amazingly, despite Jacob's wicked behavior, God did accomplish His purpose for the patriarch, passing on the covenant through him and using him to father the twelve tribes of the future nation of Israel.

We need to examine ourselves on a daily basis to see if we, in fact, are not living in like manner with Jacob when it comes to understanding our salvation and all the promises of God stored up for us in Jesus. Are we seeking to earn our place in the covenant or add to the grace of God in some measure to secure more fully our salvation? Do we think that since we are the redeemed of God, it is acceptable to use any and every means to advance our position and our worth — in Christ's kingdom and perhaps within our own perceived kingdom? The Bible makes it abundantly clear that we are saved by grace through faith, not according to works, so that no one may boast (Ephesians 2:8–9). Jacob learned this most important of truths later in his life. Let us ask the Spirit to use the Word to teach us these things today as well.

When we come to the Lord's Supper, the bread and the cup remind us that we come according to the grace of God in Christ alone, and that we bring nothing of merit before Him — nothing that can proclaim before the judgment seat of God, "I am justified!" nothing, that is, but the completed work of Christ and His righteousness — His work credited to us. The Lord's Supper is a covenant meal of grace and faith — never merit, unless we mean to speak of Christ's merit, that is. Let us pray that as we gather around the Table of our Lord, that God will deal with us and our faith-compromising, self-reliant tendencies, just as He dealt with Jacob's so long ago.

PRAYER:
O Lord our God, how often we have sought to take matters into our own hands without looking first to You. We have to confess that our lives often more closely resemble Jacob than they resemble the Lord Jesus. Help us to abandon our self-righteousness, abandon our self-reliance, and abandon our efforts at self-justification. Instead, quicken us, heavenly Father, by the Spirit, to embrace more and more, day by day reliance upon You, justification in Christ alone, and that humility which was so much a part of the mind and the ministry of Jesus during His earthly ministry. Bring us this day to the Lord's Supper table with nothing of our own to bring. As the old hymn puts it, Lord, *nothing in my hand I bring, simply to Thy cross I cling*. In the mighty name of Jesus. Amen.

13. Engaged to Be the Lord's

Then Isaac called Jacob and blessed him and directed him, "You must not take a wife from the Canaanite women. Arise, go to Paddan-aram to the house of Bethuel your mother's father, and take as your wife from there one of the daughters of Laban your mother's brother.

GENESIS 28:1–2

… she is free to be married to whom she wishes, only in the Lord.

1 CORINTHIANS 7:39b

PRINCIPLE:
The principle declared throughout the Word of God, be it the Old Testament instructions or the New Testament teachings of Christ and the Apostles, is that marriage between one man and one woman rightly takes place within the covenant context of faith. In other words, marital unions pleasing to God involve both the man and the woman belonging to the Lord's family of faith. Marriage is a creational ordinance and therefore unbelievers as well as believers are entitled, according to God's general grace, to marry. However, for those who are in Christ, only another believer is suitable as a life-long covenant help-meet.

The interesting truth for us as we prepare to approach the Lord's Table, is that in Scripture we see covenant marriage used as a metaphor, or analogy — perhaps an illustration — of the covenant relationship between Jesus Christ, the Son of God, and the redeemed people of God, the invisible Church. Thus we read in the Apostle Paul's letter to the church in Ephesus:

Wives, submit to your own husbands, as to the Lord. For the husband is the head of the wife even as Christ is the head of the church, his body, and is himself its Savior. Now as the church submits to Christ, so also wives should submit in everything to their husbands. Husbands, love your wives, as Christ loved the church and gave himself up for her, that he might sanctify her, having cleansed her by the washing of water with the word, so that he might present the church to himself in splendor, without spot or wrinkle or any such thing, that she might be holy and without blemish.

The incredible inspired beauty of these verses guides our minds and our hearts into reverent contemplation of the amazing intimacy that God has designed into the framework of redemption. As believers in Jesus Christ, we are adopted into the family of God. But we are also quite intimately united to Christ through the indwelling Holy Spirit, who is even now sanctifying us and preparing us for the glorious return of Christ — who is in fact the Bridegroom of His Church. That is the picture painted for us in Jesus' revelation to the Apostle John (Revelation 19), in which the beloved of Christ beholds the great wedding supper of the Lamb. Just as a great feast takes place whenever there is a royal wedding, so there will be the greatest of feasts at the triumphal return of Christ, when those of us who have been engaged to Him by faith will finally be united with Him in the consummation of all things — the fulfillment of the new heaven and the new earth.

And this is a key component commemorated and celebrated as we gather around the table for Communion. We are the engaged bride-to-be of Christ the Lord, undergoing preparation, sanctification, and one day, glorification, on the day of that great wedding feast of the Lamb. The Lord's Supper is a delightful foretaste, which we are privileged by God's grace to enjoy on a weekly basis. Come to the Table, Christ's delicious preview of the marriage banquet which is to come!

PRAYER:
Heavenly Father, help us to see the Lord's Supper as a sweet foretaste of the marriage supper of the Lamb. Cause us to cast aside thoughts of Communion as mere ritual or even an act of pious respect. Give us Your kingdom vision for that great day when Jesus Christ returns in glory — that day when we too will be robed in resurrection glory. And then deepen in us a holy and joyful longing for that promised day and for the unimaginable celebration that will ensue — the marriage supper of the Lamb, the wedding feast of the Lord Jesus Christ and everyone of us who make up His Bride the Church. In Jesus' name. Amen.

14. Consider the Graciousness and Abundance God Has Given to Us through Christ

And Jacob was left alone. And a man wrestled with him until the breaking of the day. When the man saw that he did not prevail against Jacob, he touched his hip socket, and Jacob's hip was put out of joint as he wrestled with him. Then he said, "Let me go, for the day has broken." But Jacob said, "I will not let you go unless you bless me." And he said to him, "What is your name?" And he said, "Jacob." Then he said, "Your name shall no longer be called Jacob, but Israel, for you have striven with God and with men, and have prevailed." Then Jacob asked him, "Please tell me your name." But he said, "Why is it that you ask my name?" And there he blessed him. So Jacob called the name of the place Peniel, saying, "For I have seen God face to face, and yet my life has been delivered."

GENESIS 32:24–30

PRINCIPLE:

Throughout the pages of the Old Testament the holiness of God and man's inability in his fallen, sinful state to draw near to the Lord's presence are common, connected themes. When men such as Moses were permitted to stand in the presence of God, it was entirely due to God's grace and provision, otherwise they would have been immediately struck down. From prophets of God to the Apostle John on Patmos, everyone brought into contact with some manifestation of the living God was utterly undone and often fell down as though dead in His awesome presence.

This episode in the life of Jacob is another interesting example of the marvelous grace the Lord chooses to bestow upon His elect covenant children. It is the most amazing thing that our holy God desires to be present among His people — His fallen, sinful people. Even in faith, we continue to be imperfect works in *sanctification process*, not yet entirely free from the effects of sin in our present state.

Yet God in Christ continues to seek us, and by His Holy Spirit dwells within us. We can indeed say along with Jacob, *I have seen God face to face, and yet my life has been delivered.* Through Jesus Christ we have been justified, and already bear the stainless garments of our Savior imputed to us. Like Jacob, despite our own sinful tendencies, we have been blessed and continue to be blessed by God as heirs of His redemptive covenant.

The Lord's Supper serves as a powerful reminder to our hearts and minds that in Christ we experience the presence of the living holy God. By His Holy Spirit, gathered as His covenant people, we meet with Yahweh around His marvelous table. Despite our own failings and our continual struggle with the remains of indwelling sin in our flesh, we are frequently dining with God, our holy and righteous King, who at the same time is our loving and gracious Deliverer. In Him we are blessed and given life everlasting. While we enjoy the presence and provision of God in Christ from day to day and week to week, Communion serves as an intensified reminder of His abiding presence and astounding provision!

PRAYER:
Dear Lord, thank You for drawing near to us through Jesus Christ and through Your Holy Spirit. We thank You for Your special presence with us when we meet together for worship and gather around Your table in celebration of Communion. We praise You for Your precious promise to all of us who believe that You will never leave us or forsake us. O, how we need that sweet and powerful reassurance as we live our day to day lives. And how very much we thank You that when we partake of the Lord's Supper we are freshly reminded of Your presence with us. Please increase our longing for You and for these times of Your special presence when we worship — when we hear Your Word proclaimed — when we eat and when we drink. In Jesus' name. Amen.

15. Redeemed and Reconciled Relationship

But Esau ran to meet him and embraced him and fell on his neck and kissed him, and they wept. And when Esau lifted up his eyes and saw the women and children, he said, "Who are these with you?" Jacob said, "The children whom God has graciously given your servant." Then the servants drew near, they and their children, and bowed down. Leah likewise and her children drew near and bowed down. And last Joseph and Rachel drew near, and they bowed down. Esau said, "What do you mean by all this company that I met?" Jacob answered, "To find favor in the sight of my lord." But Esau said, "I have enough, my brother; keep what you have for yourself." Jacob said, "No, please, if I have found favor in your sight, then accept my present from my hand. For I have seen your face, which is like seeing the face of God, and you have accepted me. Please accept my blessing that is brought to you, because God has dealt graciously with me, and because I have enough." Thus he urged him, and he took it.
GENESIS 33:4–11

PRINCIPLE:
This account from the life of Jacob serves to remind us of the importance God assigns to the bonds of family and the exhortation to, *If possible, so far as it depends on you, live peaceably with all* (Romans 12:18). The Patriarch Jacob had been living in Paddan-aram for 20 years, partly in an effort to put some distance between him and his older brother Esau, whom he had tricked out of both the birthright and the firstborn's blessing. Jacob had good reason to fear Esau when he left Canaan, as Esau did purpose in his heart to murder his younger brother as soon as their father Isaac was gathered to his fathers in death.

What we see as the events unfold between Jacob and Esau is that only God can bring restoration to a relationship which is destroyed by sin, deception, and murderous anger. In our own fleshly proclivities there abides no strength or even desire to effect reconciliation with those we have wronged or who have wronged us. Yet the Lord God carefully worked on Jacob's heart over a twenty-year period, and from the text there are indications that He also changed Esau's heart in some areas relating to his troublesome younger brother. It requires the work of God — the God who reconciled us to Himself in Christ Jesus — to bring about genuine reconciliation.

And so as we come to the Lord's Feast, spread before us upon the Communion table, let us ask the Holy Spirit to work in us a renewed, refreshed, reinvigorated appreciation for the reconciliation God has accomplished for us through the perfect obedience and shed blood of Jesus Christ our Lord. In Him by faith, we are reconciled to God our Father and we are reconciled to one another as members of the same covenant family. We need the Spirit to regularly remind us of that great truth, and we need the Spirit and the Word working in us to effect reconciliation within our families — both in birth and in rebirth — when we find ourselves at odds with one another. Let us come to the Supper today as those reconciled to God in Christ, and reconciled to one another in Christ. Thanks be to God in Christ Jesus our risen and reigning Lord!

> **PRAYER:**
> Dear heavenly Father, by Your Holy Spirit please work within us a renewed awareness of the reconciliation You have accomplished for each of us who believe through the shed blood of Jesus Christ our Lord. As we come to the Supper, may we rejoice in our restored and wonderful relationship with You and also with one another within the redeemed family of Your kingdom. In Jesus' gracious name. Amen.

16. Raised to Dominion and Authority

And Pharaoh said to his servants, "Can we find a man like this, in whom is the Spirit of God?" Then Pharaoh said to Joseph, "Since God has shown you all this, there is none so discerning and wise as you are. You shall be over my house, and all my people shall order themselves as you command. Only as regards the throne will I be greater than you." And Pharaoh said to Joseph, "See, I have set you over all the land of Egypt."

GENESIS 41:38–41

PRINCIPLE:
The account of God's amazing work in the life of Joseph is one of great suffering and trial, culminating in exaltation and absolute authority. This afflicted slave and prisoner is elevated, through a divinely appointed chain of events, to the seat of dominion over the most powerful nation of that time. And God used Joseph mightily to preserve the lives of His chosen people — Jacob and his sons and their families — from the devastating famine that was about to come. Joseph's elevation by God's providential plan and according to His grace also reminds us of the influential political office the Lord gave to His servant Daniel in the Neo-Babylonian Empire. Both were mighty instruments of God for His glory and for the preservation of His covenant people.

There is much in the life of Joseph that reveals a pattern in God's redemptive work. Nowhere is the pattern of great suffering and trial, followed by exaltation and dominion more clearly displayed than in the life, death, resurrection, ascension, and re-enthronement of Jesus Christ. The Lord Jesus became the Suffering Servant foretold by Isaiah. He was unjustly accused, betrayed by His own people and a close associate, and He suffered arrest, confinement, torture, and ultimately an undeserved death — doing so in our place.

But eternally more so than with Joseph, after His death, God the Father raised Jesus from the dead and received Him back into His heavenly throne room. The Son of God was restored to His place of glory and dominion at the right hand of power of the heavenly Father. And it is from that high and lofty place that He reigns over His expanding kingdom. Through His work and His authority, all the chosen people of God are preserved — not simply from starvation — but from eternal damnation.

As we gather around the Lord's Table today, let us, as the redeemed and eternally preserved people of God, remember the sufferings, trials, and atoning death of Jesus. Let us also celebrate joyfully His glorious resurrection and ascension. And let us declare the praises of the Son of God, exalted anew in His Father's heavenly throne chamber, and who even now reigns over His kingdom at the Father's mighty right hand!

PRAYER:

Our gracious and loving heavenly Father, we marvel at the powerful and wondrous way in which You brought Your servant Joseph from the depths of prison to the heights of political power in Egypt. Yet it is far more astounding to us that You sent Your one and only Son from the place of honor at Your right hand into the lowliest estate in this world in order to serve us and to give His life a ransom for many. We praise You that after the Lord Jesus had finished the servant-work You gave Him to do, that You raised Him gloriously from the dead and restored Him to that place of greatest honor at Your right hand. And further we thank and honor You that You bestowed upon Him that name which is above every name, that at the name of Jesus, every knee will bow and every tongue confess that He is Lord! We make this prayer in the name of Jesus, Who alone is King of kings and Lord of lords. Amen.

17. The Passover and the Supper I

And you shall eat it in haste. It is the Lord's Passover. For I will pass through the land of Egypt that night, and I will strike all the firstborn in the land of Egypt, both man and beast; and on all the gods of Egypt I will execute judgments. I am the Lord. The blood shall be a sign for you, on the houses where you are. And when I see the blood, I will pass over you, and no plague will befall you to destroy you, when I strike the land of Egypt. This day shall be for you a memorial day, and you shall keep it as a feast to the Lord; throughout your generations, as a statute forever, you shall keep it as a feast.

Exodus 12:11–14

PRINCIPLE:

The Lord instituted the feast of Passover as a perpetual reminder for the people. Year after year, the Passover visibly displayed God's covenantal faithfulness and His mighty deliverance of Israel from slavery in Egypt. Yahweh proved Himself true and trustworthy in fulfilling His great promises to the sons of Abraham, and He proved Himself to be utterly and eternally committed to His chosen people. Through the provision of the blood of the Passover lambs, God provided for the deliverance of the Hebrews, while bringing terrible judgment upon all of the firstborns among the Egyptians.

The tribes of Israel celebrated the Passover with a specific menu — items such as unleavened bread, roasted lamb, a cup of blessing. By the first century era and the years of Jesus' teaching ministry, the Passover featuring these items was a long-established visual testimony of God's faithfulness to His people. The bread, the lamb, and the wine of the cup of blessing all acted as visual and tactile symbols of the Lord as Redeemer.

It is indeed fitting that Jesus Christ, whose shed blood delivers us from certain death and judgment, instituted the Lord's Supper during His celebration of the Passover with His disciples on the night He was betrayed and turned over to death. Just as the Hebrews were commanded to keep the Passover feast in perpetual reminder and thanksgiving for their mighty deliverance from slavery in Egypt, so also we today who believe in Christ are instructed to keep the Lord's Supper feast perpetually, celebrating our deliverance from bondage to sin and death through the shed blood of our Passover Lamb, Jesus.

PRAYER:

Lord Jesus Christ, I thank You that You are my Passover Lamb, whose shed blood covers all of my sin and stays the hand of judgment which I rightly deserve to receive from the Father. Precious Savior, I thank You that You instituted this new Passover feast — Your Supper — in order to remind me again and again of Your faithfulness to the promises of the Covenant of Redemption and of Your great love set upon me.

Help me to draw near to You spiritually through the physical elements of the bread and the cup, which are Your symbolic signposts ever pointing to Christ Jesus and His Passover sacrifice to deliver me from eternal slavery to sin. I praise You for setting me feet upon that pathway of faith that leads our of captivity into Your Promised Land.

Father, Son, and Holy Spirit, help me I pray to walk in a manner worthy of this great deliverance from slavery to sin and death which You have provided for me. Work within me also an abiding love and appreciation for the delights and edifications You work in me through the celebration of Communion with You. Help me to long for this worshipful meal and the fullness of its blessings to me as Your Gospel Feast. In Jesus' name, Amen.

18. The Passover and the Supper II

> *Unleavened bread shall be eaten for seven days; no leavened bread shall be seen with you in all your territory. You shall tell your son on that day, 'It is because of what the Lord did for me when I cam out of Egypt.' And it shall be to you a sign on your hand and as a memorial between your eyes, that the law of the Lord may be in your mouth. For with a strong hand the Lord has brought you out of Egypt. You shall therefore keep this statute at its appointed time from year to year.*
>
> EXODUS 13:7–20

PRINCIPLE:

People often wonder how churches today choose the visible form of bread for use in their Lord's Supper celebrations. While practices vary from denomination to denomination, and even from congregation to congregation, many churches choose unleavened bread for observing Communion. The practice in Judaism right up to the present day and extending back to the original institution of Passover by God during the Exodus features unleavened bread. We are told in Moses' account of the first Passover that the Lord instructed unleavened bread be used not only for the Passover evening, but for the seven days associated with Passover known as the Feast of Unleavened Bread. This unleavened bread reminded the people that they departed from Egypt in great haste. Unleavened bread also came to be associated with purity, or a symbol for lack of sinfulness.

As Jesus instituted the Lord's Supper during the Passover Feast with His disciples, He told them that the unleavened bread at the Table which He had blessed and broken represented His own body, *which is given for you* (Luke 22:19). It is fitting that unleavened Passover bread was used by Christ to visibly remind His disciples of the work He was about to accomplish, in taking upon His shoulders — His body — the sins which rightly belonged to us, while hanging upon that cruel cross. Many believers also note that the unleavened bread borrowed from the Jewish Passover which many churches use for Communion, also has numerous piercings and stripes. As such, it further makes an effective visual statement reminding us of the scourging Jesus received and also of the nails that pierced His sinless hands and feet. As we celebrate the Supper, whatever form of bread is used, let us recall that the bread serves to bring to our minds and hearts the sinless body of

Christ, which became sin in our place, that we might become in Him the righteousness of God.

> **PRAYER:**
> Heavenly Father, Lord of all and Deliverer of Your chosen people, thank You for the perfect sinlessness of Jesus Christ Your Son, whom You willingly sent to suffer and horribly die upon the cross of Calvary. Thank You for His body, represented by the bread in Communion, which bore my awful transgressions upon the tree! Thank You that the foreshadows of the Passover were perfectly and eternally fulfilled in Your one and only Son, Who truly is the Paschal Lamb of God Who takes away the sin of the world! Help me now, O God, by the working of Your Spirit, to behold and to partake of the benefits of the body of Christ as I receive the bread provided at Your Table. In Jesus' sinless name I pray, Amen.

19. You Will Bring Them In

> *"You have led in your steadfast love the people whom you have redeemed; you have guided them by your strength to your holy abode.... You will bring them in and plant them on your own mountain, the place, O Lord, which you have made for your abode, the sanctuary, O Lord, which your hands have established. The Lord will reign forever and ever."*
>
> Exodus 15:13, 17–18

PRINCIPLE:

The victory song of Moses is one of many great hymns of praise and thanksgiving to God found in the Bible. The events which inspired Moses to exult in the Lord included God's miraculous work in bringing Israel out of bondage in Egypt and His amazing deliverance of the Hebrew tribes from Pharaoh's pursuing chariots by dividing the waters of the Red Sea and permitting His people to cross on dry ground.

And Moses, moved by the Spirit of the Lord, was also able to see that God redeemed His people from slavery in Egypt with a specific purpose in mind for them. That purpose was to bring the Hebrew tribes first to Mt. Sinai and then ultimately to Mt. Zion in the Promised Land. The one true God, Yahweh, saved the descendants of Abraham, Isaac, and Jacob in faithfully keeping His covenant promises in order to draw them close to Him in praise, worship, and adoration. God was going to make of Israel a *kingdom of priests and a holy nation* (Exodus 19:6).

The same fundamental principle is at work today in the life of everyone who believes in the name of Jesus. God has sent His Son, Who died on the cross as our substitute and purchased our redemption from eternal condemnation in hell and slavery to sin. By the Holy Spirit and the gift of faith, Jesus now leads us along the wilderness path in this life, to places of covenantal community worship, praise, and adoration. And at the end of our journey in this life, the Lord brings us into His immediate presence while we await the new Promised Land — the new heaven and earth — which we will inherit at Jesus' glorious return.

Long ago, Moses led the people of God in joyful, exuberant worship in praise of the Lord, their Redeemer. And today God calls His people to gather in celebration each Lord's Day to give praise and thanksgiving to Him and to the Son and to the Spirit. We come together for Sabbath worship in order to give glory to God and to give thanks and praise to Jesus, our Redeemer. How very sweet it is for the covenant family of God to join together in celebration of the God of our salvation!

Moses and the people of Israel could see the tokens of God's amazing salvation spread out before them along the shore of the Red Sea. The deliverance had been accomplished and yet the symbols remained clearly visible for everyone to see. This is also the case when we include the Lord's Supper in our Sabbath worship celebrations. Displayed before us are the symbolic tokens of our eternal salvation in Christ — the bread and the cup — which serve to remind us of Jesus' sin-bearing body and sin-cleansing blood.

> **PRAYER:**
> O Lord, our Lord, how majestic is Your name in all of the earth! We rejoice today even as Moses and the tribes of Israel did so long ago in the God of our salvation. We thank You and praise You for redeeming us from slavery to sin and condemnation in the fires of hell for eternity. We give You honor and glory for leading us along the path in this life which brings us into regular seasons of worship and adoration as Your people, delighted by the joy of our salvation in Jesus. We thank You that as we worship and sing and praise and hear from Your Word, we also see before us the beautiful tokens of the bread and the cup, which remind us of the great salvation we have received by Your grace through Christ, Your Son. Increase our joy and jubilation in You this day! Enlarge our hearts with gladness and fullness in the eternal deliverance which You have made for us in Jesus Christ, in Whose name we pray. Amen.

20. Manna from Heaven and the Supper

> *Then the Lord said to Moses, "Behold, I am about to rain bread from heaven for you, and the people shall go out and gather a day's portion every day, that I may test them, whether they will walk in my law or not. Now the house of Israel called its name manna. It was like coriander seed, white, and the taste of it was like wafers made with honey. Moses said, "This is what the Lord has commanded: 'Let an omer of it be kept throughout your generations, so that they may see the bread with which I fed you in the wilderness, when I brought you out of the land of Egypt.'"*
> Exodus 16:4, 31–32

PRINCIPLE:
The visible bread used for celebrating the Lord's Supper may vary in many different ways, from one church to another just down the same street, yet the meaning symbolized by the bread remains consistent. Just as the manna from heaven symbolized God's provision for His chosen people during the time of the Exodus, so now the bread used in the Lord's Supper symbolizes for us the true heavenly bread — *the living bread that came down from heaven* (John 6:51a) — that is, Jesus Christ, the bread of life. Just as the omer of manna served to remind the people of their deliverance from bondage in Egypt and the provision for their hunger that the Lord had made, so now the bread of Communion serves to regularly remind us of our deliverance from slavery to sin and the provision of God for our spiritual hunger, through the flesh of Jesus, the Son of Man.

    The Bible also reveals that the manna rained down from heaven through God's lovingkindness not simply for one day, or six days out of seven for one week. And it did not stop after a full year's worth of weeks. In fact God provided such miraculous food for some forty years — the entire time from the forty-fifth day of the first year out of Egypt until the day when the people of God camped at the border of the Promised Land!

    Now, just as God's provision of miraculous manna bread was always provided to His people as they walked the journey of faith between their freedom from slavery in Egypt to the day they entered into the land of His promise, so also the Lord gives us the true living manna of Jesus Christ, His Son, not just once at the moment of our salvation, but always — daily, constantly, as we also walk along our wilderness way of faith from salvation to His glorious Promised Land. Jesus promised us that, *If anyone eats of this bread, he will live forever. And the bread that I will give for the life of the world is my flesh* (John 6:51b). To eat of Jesus' bread is to believe in His name and to walk by faith in Jesus, by God's Word, and through the Holy Spirit. This is symbolized and spiritually and truly communicated to us when we receive the bread and the cup of the Lord's Supper.

PRAYER:

Gracious heavenly Father, thank you for the visible signs You give to me and to all of Your people, which proclaim Your faithfulness in providing for deliverance from the chains and curse of sin, remind us of the willing work of Jesus Your Son in offering His body upon the cross, and declare Your eternal provision of grace for us as we come as Your invited guests to the Supper. Thank you for raining down upon us by Your Holy Spirit the living bread we daily need, the heavenly manna, which is Jesus Christ, Your Son and our Lord. May we come often to Your bountiful Table, as those whose spirits need refreshing and whose faith-hunger needs to be satisfied through the heavenly bread of Christ. Help us as we partake to truly not live by physical bread alone, but by every Word that proceeds from Your mouth, and also by the Word made flesh, the living bread, Jesus Christ. In Whose name we pray. Amen.

21. The Covenant Meal and the Supper

> *And Moses took the blood and threw it on the people and said, "Behold the blood of the covenant that the Lord has made with you in accordance with all these words." Then Moses and Aaron, Nadab, and Abihu, and seventy of the elders of Israel went up, and they saw the God of Israel. There was under his feet as it were a pavement of sapphire stone, like the very heaven for clearness. And he did not lay his hand on the chief men of the people of Israel; they beheld God, and ate and drank.*
>
> EXODUS 24:8–11

PRINCIPLE:

Through the shed blood which sealed the covenant between the Lord and the Hebrews at Mt. Sinai, the leaders and seventy elders of Israel were admitted to table fellowship with the God of Israel. They and the people had been sprinkled with the blood of the sacrifice and they had accepted the Lord's covenant. The fellowship that had been forbidden just hours before — upon pain of death — was now an amazing reality by means of the covenant sealed in sacrificial blood. The fear and dread of the people at the foot of Mt. Sinai at even the sound of God's voice was replaced with confidence to enter into immediate fellowship with the one eternal God — Yahweh, the living God of Israel. The Lord had transformed the people's very real fear of certain death into a new and living hope, based upon close fellowship with their creator and deliverer.

The Lord's Supper is also a covenant meal. We, who were formerly cut off from fellowship with God and covered with sin, are instead covered by the shed blood of Christ, sealed into the covenant, and admitted into intimate communion with the great King of glory! Through Jesus by faith we have access to the heavenly Father's family dining table. Whereas we once were under a sentence of death for sin, we now hold a certificate of adoption as the Lord's own sons and daughters! As the author of Hebrews 12:17–24 declares: *For you have not come to what may be touched, a blazing fire and darkness and gloom and a tempest and the sound of a trumpet and a voice whose words made the hearers beg that no further messages be spoken to them. For they could not endure the order that was given, "If even a beast touches the mountain, it shall be stoned." Indeed, so terrifying was the sight that Moses said, "I tremble with fear." But you have come to Mount Zion and to the city of the living God, the heavenly Jerusalem, and to innumerable angels in festal gathering, and to the assembly of the firstborn who are enrolled in heaven, and to God, the judge of all, and to the spirits of the righteous made perfect, and to Jesus, the mediator of a new covenant, and to the sprinkled blood that speaks a better word than the blood of Abel.*

Table fellowship with God through the Spirit of Christ during the Gospel Feast is a precious privilege that we dare not ever take for granted. We are as welcome in the Father's presence, through His Son, as is Jesus Himself, for when the Father looks at us, He sees the covering of the blood of Christ. This is one family meal we dare not miss or dismiss.

PRAYER:

God of Moses, God of Israel, God of the covenant, and my God and Sovereign, I thank You for the shed blood of Jesus, which seals to me by faith the benefits of the Covenant of Redemption and all of your wonderful promises to Your adopted children. Thank You for inviting and admitting me and all those You love to Your heavenly dining table. To think that I can enjoy an even fuller privilege of communion with You than those who ate and drank the covenant meal at Sinai! Through Christ, You invite me to dine with You, not once, or twice, or even three times — but always and forever, and represent this to me through the visible elements of the bread and wine of the Supper. Father, I know that in myself I am unworthy of appearing before Your presence and taking a seat at Your excellent table. Thank You that I am counted worthy, though, entirely worthy, through the perfect one-time sacrifice of Jesus, Your Son. In whose name I pray, Amen.

22. Jesus, Our Atonement and the Supper

> *Then he shall kill the goat of the sin offering that is for the people and bring its blood inside the veil and do with its blood as he did with the blood of the bull, sprinkling it over the mercy seat and in front of the mercy seat. Thus he shall make atonement for the Holy Place, because of the uncleanness of the people of Israel and because of their transgressions, all their sins.... No one may be in the tent of meeting from the time he enters to make atonement in the Holy Place until he comes out and has made atonement for himself and for his house and for all the assembly of Israel.*
>
> LEVITICUS 16:15, 17

PRINCIPLE:

The Day of Atonement was arguably the single most important day on the Jewish calendar. If anything should have gone wrong during the careful observance of all the sacrifices and rituals required, the people of Israel, rather than enjoying both cleansing and removal of sanctions for their sin, would have remained in their sins, bearing their own guilt and shame for another year. And of course, with each passing day following the Day of Atonement, their sins began to accumulate during the new year.

Through Jesus Christ, the Day of Atonement has indeed been completely fulfilled for all who believe in Him alone for salvation. Through Jesus, our uncleanness has been purged away. Through Jesus, our justly deserved penalties and sanctions from God have been borne away — carried upon His shoulders. And this one-time atonement of Christ was eternally sufficient, as the author of Hebrews makes plain, *Nor was it to offer himself repeatedly, as the high priest enters the holy places every year with blood not his own, for then he would have had to suffer repeatedly since the foundation of the world. But as it is, he has appeared once for all at the end of the ages to put away sin by the sacrifice of himself* (Hebrews 9:25–26).

Atonement is an interesting word. It turns out this word did not exist in the English language, let alone the concept it describes. In order to create this word and to describe this annual Jewish service, the three words "at," "one," and "ment" were brought together. This term then describes this important Jewish festival and the greater work of Jesus on our behalf. Indeed through the Son's atoning death we who believe in Him are made to be *at one* with God our Lord. The separation of sin is removed and we enjoy renewed fellowship with Yahweh. This is wonderfully depicted for us and made vividly tangible to our senses during the celebration of the Lord's Supper.

> **PRAYER:**
>
> Heavenly Father, I thank You that the sacrifices and rituals of the Day of Atonement and of the other rites of the Mosaic Covenant were really shadows and signs, pointing the way to Jesus Christ, the one-time perfect sin offering for me and for all those who believe. Thank You that Jesus is our Passover and our Atonement and that His blood is the blood sprinkled upon the heavenly mercy seat. Thank You that Jesus' blood grants me and all believers access into the true Holy Place, for which the tabernacle and the temple of Israel were merely patterns and visible representations.
>
> Thank You, Lord Jesus Christ, that You have atoned for all of my sins once and for all when You suffered and died upon the cross at Calvary. And thank You that as I join my brothers and sisters around Your table for the Supper, together we remember and we celebrate Your completed offering until Your glorious return.

23. Jesus, Our Scapegoat and the Supper

> *And when he has made an end of atoning for the Holy Place and the tent of meeting and the altar, he shall present the live goat. And Aaron shall lay both his hands on the head of the live goat, and confess over it all the iniquities of the people of Israel, and all their transgressions, all their sins. And he shall put them on the head of the goat and send it away into the wilderness by the hand of a man who is in readiness. The goat shall bear all their iniquities on itself to a remote area, and he shall let the goat go free in the wilderness.*
>
> LEVITICUS 16:20–22

PRINCIPLE:

As part of the ceremony for the Day of Atonement, God instructed Moses to have Aaron *take from the congregation of the people of Israel two male goats for a sin offering, and one ram for a burnt offering.* The interesting aspect of God's directions concerning these two goats is that only one of them was to be sacrificed to Yahweh. The Lord told Moses that Aaron *shall take the two goats and set them before the Lord at the entrance of the tent of meeting. And Aaron shall cast lots over the two goats, one lot for the Lord and the other lot for Azazel.*

The goat upon which the lot fell for the Lord was to be sacrificed as a sin offering, much as other animals were offered as part of the Hebrew worship of Yahweh. However, the other goat, upon which the lot fell for Azazel, was to be kept alive and later that day set free in the wilderness. Before the goat was released by a man specially prepared for the task, the High Priest laid both his hands upon the head of the goat and confessed all of the sins of the people of Israel over it. In this way, the goat was a true scapegoat, bearing all the iniquities, transgressions, and sins of God's people and removing them from the boundaries of the camp.

In the fullest sense, Jesus Christ the Son of God is the great Scapegoat, in the sense that He bore all of the sins of those who believe in Him during the hours of His agony and death upon the cross. It is as though we laid our hands upon Him and confessed our sins, and as though He bore our sins away into the remotest of places. Yet Jesus is also the other goat — the goat of the sin offering — who died in our place. The symbolic and typological pictures portrayed for us in the two goats on the Day of Atonement are brought together in the one Person and work of Jesus Christ.

It is to this Lord Jesus that we come, as we seek Him at the Table. We come to the Suffering Servant, the Son of Man, who both bore the uncleanness of our sins and paid the penalty for our sins simultaneously upon the cross. Just as we see the rites and the reminders of Passover fulfilled in Christ, may we also see the many aspects of the Day of Atonement rituals and sacrifices once for all time achieved in Jesus' obedient and loving work for you and for me. And may we see as we are gathered around the glorious Table, first and foremost the completed and accepted atonement accomplished for us in the Son.

PRAYER:

Holy and loving heavenly Father, I know that You are perfectly holy and cannot tolerate sinfulness among Your people. Thank You that You provided for the truly faithful in Israel so long ago a means for the removal of sin's stain and a means to pay the ransom or penalty due to You for their sins. Now today, Father, I kneel before You as one, who like the people of old, have been marked out as Your chosen seed and yet continue to fall into sin. I again today plead the atoning blood of Jesus Your Son for cleansing me from sin, and I also glorify Christ for bearing my sins away, just as the scapegoat bore them away for Your people so long ago. And yet I know Father that Jesus accomplished this once and for all and that the full Day of Atonement occurred one time when Your Son died upon that cross.

Loving Father, Son, and Holy Spirit, I thank You that Your love for me perfectly met the demands of Your holiness in dealing with my sin through Jesus. Great indeed are You and greatly to be praised! Help me as I come into Your presence in Communion with other men, women, and children for whom You have atoned. Open my eyes that I may thankfully see Your resolution of my uncleanness and my condemnation through the body and blood of Jesus Christ, which is represented for me in these simple elements of bread and wine. I give You all the glory, and honor, and praise for taking my sins away that terrible, yet glorious day outside the walls of Jerusalem on Mount Calvary! In Jesus, my atonement's name I pray, Amen.

24. It Is the Blood

> *For the life of the flesh is in the blood, and I have given it for you on the altar to make atonement for your souls, for it is the blood that makes atonement by the life.*
>
> LEVITICUS 17:11

PRINCIPLE:
As God brought His people out of slavery in Egypt and into covenantal commitment to Himself, He also provided the means by which His people could be saved from both the contamination and the judgment due for their sin. This was absolutely necessary in order for the Hebrew tribes to dwell with God and to be His people. God is utterly, perfectly holy. Yet all human beings are sinners. Paul declares that no one is good, *for all have sinned and fall short of the glory of God* (Romans 3:23).

The sacrificial system that God established for His people daily demonstrated to them that sin was costly and that sin required the shedding of blood to remove its stain and penalties so that the person could again enjoy communion with the most holy God. The book of Hebrews 10:4 declares that it is impossible for the blood of bulls and goats to take away sins. And so we understand that the Old Testament sacrifices, which so vividly demonstrated that *without the shedding of blood there is no forgiveness of sins* (Hebrews 9:22), did not actually bring atonement for sin. But they did point the way to Christ's shed blood, the *for all time single sacrifice for sin* (Hebrews 10:12).

The people of God under the Old Testament sacrificial system were saved by their genuine faith in the God of Israel and in His future promised Messiah, the One who was coming to pour out His life and His blood to make eternal atonement for their souls. And so you see that just as the people of Israel looked forward to God's redemption in Christ, so we now look back to God's Messiah, Jesus, and His atoning death on the cross of Calvary.

Jesus' death was absolutely necessary in order for us to be freed from the wrath and curse due for our sin. Jesus' death and His resurrection are the very heart of the Gospel. And Jesus' atoning death is at the very heart of the celebration of the Lord's Supper. The Apostle Paul declared that every time we eat of the bread and drink of the cup, we proclaim the Lord's death until He comes. Just as our preaching is not Gospel preaching without the cross of Christ and His resurrection, so also our partaking in Communion is not true participation without our remembering by faith the shedding of Christ's blood on the cross and the victory of His death and resurrection over sin's curse upon our souls. The death of Christ is at the center of the Supper, even as it is the centerpiece of the Gospel. May we all see anew each Lord's Supper, Christ crucified and raised from the dead!

> **PRAYER:**
> Heavenly Father, help us to see Christ our atonement even more clearly as we come to receive the Lord's Supper. Cause us by Your Holy Spirit to understand the costliness of our sin and the price Jesus Your Son paid to free us from its stain, its curse, and its eternal condemnation. May we more deeply grasp that it was necessary for the Son of Man to suffer and to die so that we by faith in Him may live forever more. In Jesus' mighty name we pray. Amen.

25. Abounding in Steadfast Love

And now, please let the power of the Lord be great as you have promised, saying, "The Lord is slow to anger and abounding in steadfast love, forgiving iniquity and transgression, but he will by no means clear the guilty, visiting the iniquity of the fathers on the children, to the third and the fourth generation.' Please pardon the iniquity of this people, according to the greatness of your steadfast love, just as you have forgiven this people, from Egypt until now."

NUMBERS 14:17–19

PRINCIPLE:

Numbers 14:17–19 recounts part of Moses' great intercession with the Lord in the aftermath of the bad report of the Hebrew spies returned from the Promised Land. In this wonderful work of pleading with God, Moses actually recites the Lord's own previous description of His lovingkindness, grace, and holiness in dealing with His covenant people. Of the twelve spies sent into the land, ten returned with a discouraging report and incited the people to fear the inhabitants of the land. In response to their unbelief, the Lord God threatened to wipe out the tribes of Israel and raise up a new *nation greater and mightier than they*.

Yahweh, the faithful God of Israel listened to Moses' intercession and relented from the disaster He was going to bring upon the Hebrew tribes. While the Lord swore according to His glory that none of the men who had tested Him ten times or who had not obeyed His voice would see the land of His promise, their children would enter and possess the land.

It is in Moses' words to the Lord that we see the revelation of the forgiving character of Almighty God. And it is in the Lord's response to Moses that we also get a glimpse of His patience and His steadfast love for His chosen people. This is the consistent character of the one eternal God from everlasting to everlasting. And so He is also the faithful and gracious God we know today through Jesus Christ, His Son, our Lord and Savior.

Moses in a sense is a *type* of Christ, or a shadow of Who Christ would be when in God's timing, some fourteen hundred years after the events of Numbers 14, He would finally come. While Moses mediated between God and His people Israel in the temporal sense, Jesus the

Son of God mediated between the Lord and His covenant people for all time and every place when He went to that cross and died, serving as our great High Priest and atoning sacrifice. And even today, Christ Jesus always lives to intercede on our behalf. While His sacrificial ministry ended with His cross and His resurrection, His priestly intercession continues constantly on our behalf from His place at God the Father's right hand of power, majesty, dominion, and glory.

The forbearing, covenantal, and faithful character of God is always symbolized for us in the bread and the cup of the Lord's Supper. This is because Jesus Christ is the exact imprint of the God the Father and He radiates the Father's glorious character in His life, ministry, death, resurrection, and priestly intercession on our behalf. And so as we come to the Sacrament, we are reminded of Christ's work as our High Priestly intercessor in the past, in the present, and for all of eternity future.

PRAYER:

Heavenly Father, please grant us, according to Your grace and through the intercession of Jesus Your Son, the blessings of Your covenant people. Forgive us our many iniquities according to the greatness of Your steadfast love toward us in Christ Jesus. Help us to see the grace and the gloriousness of Your holy character in the symbols of Jesus Christ, which are the bread and the cup of our Communion celebration. And it is in the name of our great High Priest, Jesus, that we pray. Amen.

26. The Lord Your God Is with You Wherever You Go!

"Just as I was with Moses, so I will be with you. I will not leave you or forsake you. Be strong and courageous, for you shall cause this people to inherit the land that I swore to their fathers to give them. Only be strong and very courageous, being careful to do according to all the law that Moses my servant commanded you. Do not turn from it to the right hand or to the left, that you may have good success wherever you go. This Book of the Law shall not depart from your mouth, but you shall meditate on it day and night, so that you may be careful to do according to all that is written in it. For then you will make your way prosperous, and then you will have good success. Have I not commanded you? Be strong and courageous. Do not be frightened, and do not be dismayed, for the LORD your God is with you wherever you go."

Joshua 1:5b–9

PRINCIPLE:

I don't know about you, but I need to hear God's reassuring words on a daily basis. I need to know that whatever I am facing on a given day or week or even at the start of a new year, the Lord is with me. Joshua needed God's reassurance more than three thousand years ago when he was about to lead the Hebrew tribes into the Promised Land. There were heavily fortified cities, vast well-trained armies, and giants in the land which had to be conquered. The days ahead would be filled with challenges of every kind, as well as triumphs and trials galore. Yet no matter what lay ahead, Joshua and the people had the certain promise of Yahweh's presence and His blessing. Wherever the presence of the Lord rests upon His chosen people, there is blessing, and as God puts it in Joshua 1, there is a prosperous way and good success. I am always encouraged when I read these words of promise from God and I hope that you are as well today. For in the Lord Jesus Christ these promises of God are ours as well as Joshua's!

One of the ways all of us are reminded and encouraged about God's promise to be with us and to never leave us or forsake us is through our weekly celebration of the Lord's Supper. When received in addition to the revelation and proclamation of God's Word, Communion is used by the Holy Spirit to remind us and assure us of the Lord's abiding presence among us and within us. The Supper highlights this intimate relationship with God our Father through Christ Jesus His Son. It also underscores for us that Jesus loved us so deeply He was willing to give His life as a ransom for each and every one of us who believe in Him. And through the Holy Spirit, the Lord Jesus abides with us continually. All of this and much more is represented for us when we share together in the Lord's Supper as part of our weekly Sunday worship celebration.

PRAYER:

Our gracious and loving heavenly Father, please cause your Holy Spirit to use Your revealed Word and the Sacrament of the Lord's Supper today to remind us of Your constant and powerful presence. May each of us hear from the Spirit of God anew, just as Joshua did so long ago, *Be strong and courageous. Do not be frightened, and do not be dismayed, for the LORD your God is with you wherever you go.* We thank You that through the constant presence of the Spirit of Christ, you are indeed always with us wherever we go in this life of faith. In the name of the Father, and the Son, and the Holy Spirit. Amen.

27. Communion as Covenant Renewal Celebration

At that time Joshua built an altar to the Lord, the God of Israel, on Mount Ebal, just as Moses the servant of the Lord had commanded the people of Israel, as it is written in the Book of the Law of Moses, "an altar of uncut stones, upon which no man has wielded an iron tool." And they offered on it burnt offerings to the Lord and sacrificed peace offerings. And there, in the presence of the people of Israel, he wrote on the stones a copy of the law of Moses, which he had written. And all Israel, sojourner as well as native born, with their elders and officers and their judges, stood on opposite sides of the ark before the Levitical priests who carried the ark of the covenant of the Lord, half of them in front of Mount Gerizim and half of them in front of Mount Ebal, just as Moses the servant of the Lord had commanded at the first, to bless the people of Israel. And afterward he read all the words of the law, the blessing and the curse, according to all that is written in the Book of the Law. There was not a word of all that Moses commanded that Joshua did not read before all the assembly of Israel, and the women, and the little ones, and the sojourners who lived among them.

JOSHUA 8:30–31

PRINCIPLE:

Here in Joshua chapter 8, the Israelites have again received a mighty victory under the banner of Yahweh over the people of Ai. Immediately after the great triumph, Joshua leads the people of God in a great covenant renewal ceremony. During this celebration of God's covenant with His people, the words of the Lord are recorded and read in their entirety before the people. Sacrifices are also offered before the Lord. And, as this is a covenant ceremony like the previous one between the mountains in the days of Moses, we can assume that the people were required to swear an oath to enter into God's gracious covenant.

The same thing actually takes place every Lord's Day when we are all gathered as God's covenant people for worship. We receive the written Word of God, read and explained to us through the proclamation of the preacher and the various passages read. We also confess anew our commitment to live in the Covenant of Redemption by faith in Christ. And we celebrate the covenant that Christ sealed for us in Him as we draw near to share in the Lord's Supper.

What a marvelous privilege and blessing the Lord gives to us! We have a covenant renewal celebration in the victory of Jesus each and every Lord's Day as we worship and receive God's means of grace. What a wonderful and abundantly providing God we serve! May the Spirit of Christ lead us all in a joyful renewal of our covenant participation each Lord's Day as we hear the Word, sing God's praises, and gather around Christ's table.

PRAYER:

Heavenly Father, help us to see with eyes of faith that our worship, including our Lord's Supper celebrations, are much more than religious rituals that mark time during our sojourn of faith in this life. Please open our hearts and minds to see that every service of worship and every Lord's Supper represent the renewal of Your covenant with us in Jesus Christ. Cause us to hunger and thirst for the satisfying refreshment that only comes when we as adopted children are gathered together in Your Fatherly presence. In Jesus' name. Amen.

28. Refuge in Christ and the Lord's Supper

Now therefore, O kings, be wise; be warned, O rulers of the earth. Serve the Lord with fear, and rejoice with trembling. Kiss the Son, lest he be angry, and you perish in the way, for his wrath is quickly kindled. Blessed are all who take refuge in him.
Psalm 2:10–13

PRINCIPLE:
When we read Psalm 2, it is natural for us to apply its revealed truths to those who are divinely called to positions of authority over our city, our state, or our nation. Indeed, the psalmist does address kings and rulers in verses 1, 2, and 10. However, we must also take note that the psalm's instruction applies equally to each and every human being. Psalm 2 begins with a direct address to groups of persons — *nations*, and *peoples*. Admittedly, the inspired aim of the psalmist is to confront political nation-states and their ungodly rulers. Yet there is ever present in the text a consideration of each person from which these political organizations are composed. The very last line of Psalm 2 is very revealing in this regard, as it states: *Blessed are all who take refuge in him.*

Psalm 2 addresses that sinful inclination in every one of us, whether king or pauper — whether president or powerless, to rebel against the authority and ultimate rule of the King of kings and Lord of lords, Jesus Christ, the Son of the living God. The antidote, the psalm plainly declares, to our rebellious condition is to come before Jesus the Son, submit ourselves to His divine authority, and find in Him our one and only eternal refuge. In order for us to ever have the desire to turn from rebellion to obedience, the Holy Spirit of God must transform our rebellious hearts into hearts truly prepared to yield to the King of all. This is the free gift of God according to His electing love. The Father and the Son pour out the Holy Spirit upon all whose names are written in the Lamb's book of life. As the Spirit indwells the children of God, we are able to *kiss the Son.*

It is helpful for us to see in the Lord's Supper a living, Spirit-birthed symbol of the refuge we have found in Jesus. We gather around the King's Table, not as a rebellious *people plotting in vain*, but rather as God's own redeemed covenant people — *the people of his pasture and the sheep of his hand* — as Psalm 95 declares. We enter into the presence of our King and Savior *rejoicing with trembling*. And through the gift of faith and the Holy Spirit, we indeed have kissed the royal Son.

PRAYER:
Our gracious and loving heavenly Father, please help us now to truly find our refuge in You. And as we seek by faith to make You the fortress, shield, and shelter of our lives, may we also bring blessing and conviction to the civil affairs of which we are a part in this city, state, and nation. Like Joseph in Egypt, Daniel in Babylon, and Paul in Rome, may we testify of Your strength — Your power to deliver, and may we ever and always point others to Your Son, the Lord Jesus Christ, Your anointed servant and Savior. As we come to the Supper may we show our covenantal devotion and loyalty to King Jesus, Your kingly heir. And may we do so as citizens of Your kingdom, seeking to build that kingdom while subjecting the kingdoms and political systems of this world unto King Jesus. And it is in Jesus' name we pray. Amen.

29. Jesus the Good Shepherd and the Supper

You prepare a table before me in the presence of my enemies; you anoint my head with oil; my cup overflows. Surely goodness and mercy shall follow me all the days of my life, and I shall dwell in the house of the Lord forever.

PSALM 23:5–6

PRINCIPLE:

Within the most recognized among all of King David's psalms, the fourth and fifth verses of Psalm 23, we have recorded these marvelous words of confidence and hope in the abundant and faithful provision of the Lord for His covenant children. David declares that God's sustaining grace and blessings are generously bestowed upon His beloved sheep, even as we find ourselves under the spiteful gaze of our most fearful and ravenous enemies. Beyond the Lord's incredible sustaining goodness, as believers we enjoy the particular privilege of God's anointing to kingly authority as vice-regents upon the earth. The inspired psalmist adds that God's covenant faithfulness remains with us throughout the heights and the depths, for the totality of the days of our lives. Beyond all of these priceless gifts, David declares from the confident faith of his heart the certain hope we also share of eternal life in the everlasting presence of God our Lord.

As we consider Jesus' institution of the Lord's Supper on the eve of His sacrificial death, we recall that all of the blessings and comforts King David mentions in Psalm 23 derive from Christ's work on our behalf. He perfectly kept the covenant requirements that we couldn't keep and He sealed the covenant of grace and redemption in His own blood. Of course, the Lord Jesus also identified Himself as the Good Shepherd, even as he said in John 10:14, *I am the good shepherd. I know my own and my own know me.* Thanks to God's gift of saving faith, we now recognize Christ as our Good Shepherd. As Jesus describes it, *The sheep hear his voice, and he calls his own sheep by name and leads them out* (John 10:3b). This is the beautiful relationship we now enjoy because Jesus gave His life for His sheep.

When we gather together around the Table that Jesus has prepared, let us come as those whose table fellowship declares the Gospel to a watching and often hostile world. And let us also come as adopted sons and daughters of God who have been anointed as God's vice-regents by the power of the Holy Spirit, who are renewed and refreshed by His overflowing cup of blessing, that are daily sustained by His abiding presence, and that ever live and walk expectantly together as those *who will always be with the Lord* (1 Thessalonians 4:17).

> **PRAYER:**
> Dear gracious Lord, thank You for preparing for me a lavish table, loaded with the sweetness of Your abundant grace. I know that in Your holy Supper, I regularly enjoy Your redeeming love and the special presence of Your Holy Spirit. While Your goodness truly does follow me all the days of my life through Jesus, I also know that by faith I will dwell in Your house forevermore. In Jesus, my Good Shepherd's name, I pray. Amen.

30. Taste and See the Lord's Goodness in the Supper!

Oh, taste and see that the Lord is good! Blessed is the man who takes refuge in him! Oh, fear the Lord, you his saints, for those who fear him have no lack! The young lions suffer want and hunger; but those who seek the Lord lack no good thing.

PSALM 34:8–10

PRINCIPLE:
Psalm 34 is an exuberant declaration of God's goodness and His delight in delivering those who cry out to Him. Verses 8 through 10 in this marvelous psalm exhort us to draw near to the Lord and experience His impregnable protection and abundant provision. The psalmist likens Yahweh's faithfulness and care for His saints to the most lavish and satisfying of food. This metaphor is heightened in the contrast between verse 9, in which the saints of God who fear him *have no lack*, and the young lions of verse 10, who *suffer want and hunger*. The point is underlined yet again at the end of the same verse as King David declares, *those who seek the Lord lack no good thing*.

How desperately we need to hear this declaration of God's goodness in providing and protecting His redeemed children. On the one hand, we are so prone to depend upon our own abilities and resources to provide for and safeguard ourselves and our families. And the other hand, we often envy the vitality and resources of the young and the wealthy. Yet the psalmist reminds us that it is only when we seek and we take refuge in the Lord that our deepest needs and spiritual hunger will be satisfied once and for all.

Scripture repeatedly testifies that it is the true food by which we are to live, and that the Word made flesh, Jesus Christ, is the living bread that came down from heaven. Ultimately Jesus is the bread of life for which we desperately hunger. We can only be satisfied in Him. This is precisely why the Lord's Supper so effectively reminds us of Christ. As we eat the bread and drink from the cup, our dependence upon the Savior for His eternal, spiritual food is brought to mind just as surely as our body's need of food and drink.

Jesus invited His disciples to take and eat the bread, and to drink from the cup in remembrance of Him. He calls us to do the very same today as His 21st century disciples. And each time, in doing as He has instructed, we remember, we proclaim, and through His amazing grace, we continually *taste and see that the Lord is good!*

> **PRAYER:**
> Heavenly Father, by Your Spirit please work in me this day, as I draw near to the Table of Your kingdom feast. Remind me that I do not live by bread alone, but by every Word that proceeds from You. Likewise, that in Jesus I live and move and have my very being. Help me to seek You first, knowing that all the things I need in this life, physically and spiritually will be added to me according to Your lovingkindness and grace. May I this day indeed taste anew Your goodness, grace, and mercy given to me on account of Jesus! And it is in His good name that I pray. Amen.

31. Ask and the Lord Will Provide

I am the Lord your God,
Who brought you up out of the land of Egypt.
Open your mouth wide, and I will fill it.

PSALM 81:10

PRINCIPLE:
Throughout God's dealings with His covenant people in the Old Testament, He repeatedly reminded them of His faithfulness in delivering them from calamity. Indeed, of all the amazing things the Lord did for His chosen children in the centuries prior to Christ, the greatest in significance to the Jews was His powerful, miraculous work in bringing them out of hard bondage in Egypt. Here in Psalm 81, we see that this defining event in the history of the people of Israel was used by God to call them back to Him as the faithful Provider of every good thing. The people who bore the name of Yahweh could look back into history and see clearly the indisputable evidence of God's faithfulness and mercy.

The same is also true of us today as the elect people of God who have been redeemed by the blood of Jesus Christ. Believers in Jesus have received the greatest of God's redemptive works applied directly to them by means of faith. We have been delivered from much, much more dreadful bondage than the Hebrews of old in Egypt. In Christ, we — and every generation saved by faith stretching back to Adam — have passed from eternal bondage to death and damnation to hell into the blessedness of everlasting light and life. And yet, like the Jews of old, we are also tempted to suffer from *redemptive amnesia* concerning the gracious, abundant character and work of God.

The Lord's Supper serves, much like the psalm above, to remind us of the completed, redemptive work of God our Father. While Psalm 81 declares God's deliverance of Israel from Egypt, the Lord's Supper sacramentally declares visibly the deliverance of all of God's people in Christ Jesus His Son. The Holy Spirit uses the bread and the cup to remind us of the great deliverance from bondage to sin and death which Jesus accomplished for us when He died upon the cross so many centuries ago.

And the call of God to true believers in Him concerning the Supper resembles Psalm 81, in its exhortation to the people of God: *Open your mouth wide, and I will fill it.* This is a poetic way for God to say confidently to His people that they must look nowhere else but to Him for all the provision they need. Likewise there is nowhere else for us to look for eternal deliverance and provision but unto Jesus Christ, who is visibly proclaimed whenever the Lord's Supper is celebrated. As we receive the bread and the cup, let us again remember the great deliverance of God, who brought us up out of the land of sin and death, and has given us eternal life and every good gift through Christ Jesus our Lord.

> **PRAYER:**
> Our gracious and loving heavenly Father, we give thanks that You are the good Father, Who hears the cries of His children, Who encourages us to seek You, and Who provides for our needs according to Your riches in glory in Christ Jesus. We also give thanks that You answer our prayers, not always as we would expect, but always according to Your eternal fatherly care for our good and for Your great glory. In Jesus' name. Amen.

32. No Good Thing Does Christ Withhold

For the Lord God is a sun and shield;
the Lord bestows favor and honor.
No good thing does he withhold
from those who walk uprightly.
O Lord of Hosts,
blessed is the one who trusts in you!

Psalm 84:11–12

PRINCIPLE:

Psalm 84 is a beautiful psalm indeed. It is filled with lofty language of exaltation for God and the blessings of those who serve Him. This sense of devotion for the Lord and His worship is conveyed in the psalm's opening verses:

How lovely is your dwelling place, O Lord of hosts!
My soul longs, yes, faints for the courts of the Lord;
my heart and flesh sing for joy to the living God.

The psalmist is describing his longing for the regular assembly for worship of the people of God. There is no doubt that his innermost being constantly longed to be engaged in worship of the God of Abraham, Isaac, and Jacob — the one true Lord, Yahweh — the covenant God of Israel. The longing of God's people for gathering together in corporate worship near the tabernacle or the temple is a frequent theme in the Psalter, as is the theme of joyful, exuberant worship. If only believers in Jesus Christ today were so hungry and thirsty, and so expectant of the weekly corporate worship of the people of God. We all have to ask ourselves whether or not we truly anticipate or desire to be engaged in regular, corporate worship. And we must ask ourselves whether we truly expect to meet with and dialogue with the one true God during the Lord's Day worship gathering. What a privilege that the Lord our Savior actually desires us to commune with Him, to glorify His name, and to sing His praises!

While the inspired author begins his psalm in delight over the opportunity to worship the Lord in joyful praise, he concludes his psalm recounting the majesty and blessings found only in the Lord our God. Among the list of blessings described for those who trust in Him is this: *No good thing does he withhold from those who walk uprightly.* Among the many good things God provides for believers in Christ is the Sacrament of the Lord's Supper, which in fact is a means of God's grace. And we, as the Lord's redeemed children, are blessed when we approach the Lord's Table as those who genuinely, by means of faith alone, trust in Christ Jesus for everlasting life.

> **PRAYER:**
>
> Dear heavenly Father, we are amazed that You desire us to worship You. We confess that You do not need us to complete Yourself. We know that we bring nothing before You that is worthy. And yet You call us to Sabbath worship and the time that we spend in your special presence is truly our delight. In Christ Jesus You have bestowed upon us both favor and honor. Please increase our joy in gathering for worship and our anticipation of eating and drinking in the Supper. We are so thankful to You that among Your many gifts to us is the Sacrament of Communion — truly a good thing and a wonderful visible symbol of Your love for us in Jesus Your Son. And it is in His name that we pray. Amen.

33. Signs of God's Gracious Favor

But you, O Lord, are a God merciful and gracious,
slow to anger and abounding in steadfast love and faithfulness.
Turn to me and be gracious to me;
give your strength to your servant,
and save the son of your maidservant.
Show me a sign of your favor,
that those who hate me may see and be put to shame
because you, LORD, have helped me and comforted me.

PSALM 86:15–17

PRINCIPLE:

In God's gracious providence, Joseph experienced an amazing transformation in his life circumstances while living in Egypt. Within the space of less than a day, the slave and prisoner was elevated to the highest place of power and authority, second only to Pharaoh himself (Genesis 41:37–45). The psalmist King David also knew what it meant to bear affliction as God's anointed servant and future deliverer of God's people. In Psalm 86 he was inspired to appeal to the Lord.

Truly biblical prayer, such as we have before us in Psalm 86, is always built upon the certain knowledge of the character of Almighty God. Here the psalmist gives glory to God for His mercy and His abundant grace, His steadfast love and faithfulness. While David considers the evil, godless men who are afflicting him — who even seek his very life — his heart and mind are abruptly reminded of the character of Yahweh, his God.

The king's remembrance of God's lovingkindness in past trials becomes the basis for his petition that the Lord would lift his affliction at the hands of his oppressors and deliver him from trouble. He asks for strengthening. He also pointedly asks for God to show him a sign of His favor. David understood all too well the suffering and sometimes unjust affliction that comes in this life upon those who are in communion with God through the Covenant of Redemption. At the same time, the psalmist understood the unchangeable love of God toward those He has chosen. God had transformed Joseph's life and He could certainly do the same for His servant, David.

King David saw this inspired prayer answered during his lifetime. In fact, it was part of a pattern of deliverance which God provided to His servant on many occasions, through all the times of great peril the son of Jesse was appointed to endure.

Yet this inspired prayer has much wider application and import than simply the time, place, and immediate circumstances in which it was spoken. This marvelous prayer is one that any believer in Jesus Christ, bound by His blood into the Covenant of Redemption, may offer before the throne of God's majestic grace and lovingkindness.

And just as David rejoiced to see his prayer answered favorably in his day, so we as the adopted children of God can rejoice in its fulfillment for each of us through the shed blood of Jesus Christ. And while we also have many and various *signs of God's favor*, the weekly Communion we celebrate with Him is perhaps the most encouraging. As the Lord's appointed means of grace, it is also a sign empowered by the Holy Spirit, which gives us abundant strength and comfort. In Christ we indeed know the eternal favor of God!

PRAYER:
Dear Lord, please help me to see in the Lord's Supper, a sure and wonderful sign of Your good favor toward me and all who believe in Your name. Thank you for turning to me and comforting me through Jesus Christ, Your Son, Who is so beautifully symbolized in the bread and the cup. Bring to my remembrance the salvation You have worked for me and continue to strengthen me by Your Spirit. In Jesus' name. Amen.

34. Holy, Holy, Holy Is the Lord!

In the year that King Uzziah died I saw the Lord sitting upon a throne, high and lifted up; and the train of his robe filled the temple. Above him stood the seraphim. Each had six wings: with two he covered his face, and with two he covered his feet, and with two he flew. And one called to another and said:

"Holy, holy, holy is the Lord of hosts; the whole earth is full of his glory!"

And the foundations of the thresholds shook at the voice of him who called, and the house was filled with smoke. And I said: "Woe is me! For I am lost; for I am a man of unclean lips, and I dwell in the midst of a people of unclean lips; for my eyes have seen the King, the Lord of hosts!"

Then one of the seraphim flew to me, having in his hand a burning coal that he had taken with tongs from the altar. And he touched my mouth and said: "Behold, this has touched your lips; your guilt is taken away, and your sin atoned for."

ISAIAH 6:1–7

PRINCIPLE:
Here in Isaiah chapter 6, the prophet gives us a rare and revealing vision of the Lord of hosts and His perfect holiness. God's holiness fills the temple. He is so utterly holy that even the seraphim, who serve Him and praise Him constantly, must use four of their six wings to cover themselves from the pure, brilliant radiance of the Lord's holiness. Their constantly repeated description, using the thrice holy praise, magnifies Isaiah's presentation of God as entirely other — set apart, and certainly unapproachable by someone stained by sin.

Isaiah's reaction to his encounter with the presence of the living, holy God is utter despair. The prophet knows that he is unclean, unworthy, unfit, and unprepared to stand or even kneel in the presence of the King, the Lord of hosts. And yet the Lord shows His special favor to His chosen servant. One of the attending seraphim brings to Isaiah the atoning power of God, taken from the pure, refining fire of the heavenly altar. Isaiah's guilt is removed and his sin is paid for — atoned — the debt is satisfied. In the verses that follow, God commissions Isaiah to go and to speak for Him and this redeemed servant of the Lord replies, *Here I am! Send me!*

When the Lord reveals Himself to us through the Gospel of Jesus Christ, we have our own Isaiah encounter. It may not feature all of the astounding visual elements, or even the audible voice of the Lord's calling. Yet we go through much the same process of amazement, conviction, and dismay, followed by forgiveness, grace, and commission. As the Spirit of God gives us faith and the eyes and ears to finally see and hear the Good News of Jesus Christ, we come to realize how very holy God our Father really is and how utterly stained and broken we are in His holy sight as the worst of sinners. Then, just as we are about to be overwhelmed by our guilt, shame, and separation before God, He intervenes and declares to us that the blood of Christ has been applied to us and that we are cleansed, forgiven, and *atoned for*.

The struggle we face as not yet fully sanctified believers is that we often forget in our daily lives that we have had this eternally transforming encounter with the holy, living God. And we need to constantly live and move and have our being in this life, in light of this redeeming encounter with God in Christ. One of the most effective ways to keep what Jesus has done for us always before us is to come frequently to the Lord's Table. Every time we celebrate this Sacrament we enjoy real spiritual fellowship with God in Christ. There is a sense in which we relive, or at least are vividly reminded, of that first encounter we experienced with the King, the Lord of hosts, when we came to Christ by the gift of faith. The covenant meal of the Lord's Supper is a regular memory-jogger, a constant reminder of who we once were, what Jesus has done for us, and who we therefore are now because of Him. We are also like Isaiah, reminded that we have been saved for a purpose — called to go and make disciples of all the nations — sharing the good news of Jesus' eternal, life-changing power with anyone and everyone we meet in this life.

PRAYER:

Our gracious heavenly Father, by Your Spirit please remind us as we come to the Supper of that first encounter we had with You. Convict us anew of our hopeless, sinful condition before you brought us to Yourself. Encourage us afresh of our new status as men and women who have been atoned for, forgiven, restored, adopted into Your eternal family, accepted now and always in Christ Jesus our Lord. And also rekindle in us a joy and an eagerness to go and to fulfill our Great Commission calling to share the Gospel with all the nations! In Jesus' name. Amen.

35. God Is With Us

Therefore, the Lord himself will give you a sign. Behold, the virgin will conceive and bear a son, and you shall call his name Immanuel.

Isaiah 7:14

PRINCIPLE:
More than seven hundred years prior to the birth of the Lord Jesus Christ, His coming as the Messiah of God was prophesied by Isaiah. The circumstances of this birth were to be divinely miraculous. The very Son of God, the radiance of His glory and the exact imprint of His nature, would one day come to dwell among His people in human flesh. That would have been astounding enough. Yet Jesus' incarnation was a miracle of prophetic fulfillment — the prophecy that a virgin would conceive and bear Him.

This is precisely how God brought about the sending of Jesus His Son into the world in which we live. When the angel Gabriel appears to a young woman, named Mary, she asks the heavenly messenger, *How can this be, since I am a virgin?* The angel replied, *The Holy Spirit will come upon you, and the power of the Most High will overshadow you; therefore the child to be born will be called holy — the Son of God* (Luke 1:26–38).

When we focus upon these miraculous events during the Christmas season, or at any time of the year, we are reminded that the Lord Jesus Christ was sent into the world by means of the working of His Holy Spirit, in and through the human vessel of Mary. While we do not give unusual place to Mary as Catholics do, we nevertheless accord her the same honor as does the angel Gabriel, when he refers to her as *favored one*.

The particular and providential means that God chose to bring about Jesus' birth serve to identify Him with us — the created human beings He came to save. He is like us in every respect, yet without sin. And of course, He is set apart in the sense of His eternal divinity. Yet, Jesus the Son of God is also the Son of Man. He is, as Isaiah names Him, "Immanuel," the God Who is with us.

Christ's identification with us — His willingness to take the form of a servant and to deliver us from sin, death, and hell — is the key to His substitutionary, atoning work as our Passover Lamb. This is underlined for us multiple times in the words of institution and the shared elements of the bread and the cup when we celebrate Communion. Partaking with other believers in the Lord's Supper reminds us that we profess faith in the God who sent His one and only Son to be our Immanuel, that through Jesus and by His Spirit — God indeed was, and remains, with His saved people. And so as we remember and rejoice in Christ through the Supper, we remember that ever and always He is with us.

PRAYER:

Heavenly Father, we praise You for sending Your Son Jesus to be with us, our Immanuel. We give You thanks that according to Your divine plan the Lord Jesus was both perfectly God and perfectly man. How wonderfully You worked all things together so that Jesus was like us in every way, yet without sin. Therefore He alone was fit to be our substitute when He died on that cross — a sinless God-man bearing all our sins away. We also thank You holy Father, that when You received Jesus back into the heavenly places after His resurrection, You continued Your presence with us by sending Your good Holy Spirit. In Jesus' precious name. Amen.

36. The Lord's Supper as Kingdom Celebration

> *For to us a child is born, to us a son is given; and the government shall be upon his shoulder, and his name shall be called Wonderful Counselor, Mighty God, Everlasting Father, Prince of Peace. Of the increase of his government and of peace there will be no end, on the throne of David and over his kingdom, to establish it and to uphold it with justice and with righteousness from this time forth and forevermore. The zeal of the LORD of hosts will do this.*
>
> ISAIAH 9:6–7

PRINCIPLE:
So often during the Christmas celebrations we recite this truly wonderful promise from the inspired hand of Isaiah. Its sublime yet lofty titles for the promised Son captivate our attention and give rise to a certain quiet reverence and awe. Indeed in these royal and divine titles we see the very image of Christ, who is fully the Wonderful Counselor, Mighty God, Everlasting Father, and Prince of Peace.

And yet this glorious passage begins with another highly significant truth about God's own Son. Expressed in the phrase, *and the government shall be upon his shoulder*, is the declaration that this Suffering Servant Son of God, is also the King of all. Now in order for someone to hold the title of king, he must in fact have a kingdom to rule. This is even much more so the case when someone bears the title King of kings and Lord of lords!

And what of this Christ kingdom? The prophet reveals to us, *of the increase of his government and of peace there will be no end... from this time forth and forevermore.* The emphatic declaration here is one of a kingdom that begins with the birth of this miraculous Son and then expands continually into eternity! Isaiah doesn't declare a kingdom that starts and stops, not even one that advances and retreats, but rather a kingdom that continuously increases forevermore. King Jesus' authority and the kingdom over which He reigns is ever-growing, ever-advancing, and ever-increasing. And this is so according to Scripture even during those times when our eyes look about us and we doubt and we worry over its present state.

And so as we come to the Table of the Lord with these truths in mind, let us come with joyful hearts — joyful not only for the birth of Christ, but also for the kingly reign of Christ and for His glorious kingdom upon this earth. After all, we gather around the Table of the King of kings, and we do so as His redeemed and adopted vice-regents, designated to sit with Him upon His throne, and appointed to reign with Him in light!

PRAYER:

Dear God and Father, we acknowledge with grateful hearts that Your Son Jesus is truly God, one with You. You have made it so clear through Isaiah in the revelation of some of Jesus' titles — *Wonderful Counselor, Mighty God, Everlasting Father, Prince of Peace*. We give glory and honor to You and to the Son, who is declared by You to be King — the King — ruling over a kingdom which is ever-increasing and certain to prevail. Your Word tells us that not even the gates of hell can prevail against it. What amazing reassurance this gives us. And what a privilege You have given us that we are invited to dine at Your kingly table. May we never take your invitation or this wonderful blessing for granted. May we in fact long more and more as time passes by to join in table fellowship with King Jesus and with our fellow redeemed citizens of Your prevailing kingdom. In Jesus' name. Amen.

37. He Was Pierced for Our Transgressions

He was despised and rejected by men; a man of sorrows, and acquainted with grief; and as one from whom men hide their faces he was despised, and we esteemed him not.

Surely he has borne our griefs and carried our sorrows; yet we esteemed him stricken, smitten by God, and afflicted.

But he was pierced for our transgressions; he was crushed for our iniquities; upon him was the chastisement that brought us peace, and with his wounds we are healed.

All we like sheep have gone astray; we have turned — every one — to his own way; and the Lord has laid on him the iniquity of us all.

Isaiah 53:3–6

PRINCIPLE:

Through the Spirit of God, the prophet Isaiah received a revelation of the coming Messiah of God as a suffering servant. While Jews typically thought of their coming Messianic figure as a king and perhaps a great priest, they failed to see Him as God intended and revealed through Isaiah — one Who would bear our sins, suffer, and die before He would wear the eternal crown of victory and sit upon the throne of David for all the coming ages. Isaiah described Jesus' substitutionary sufferings and death as if he had been there to Jerusalem to see it for himself. And he did so accurately, thanks to the Holy Spirit, more than seven hundred years before the events actually happened as part of God's redemptive plan!

What great and glorious Good News is contained in Isaiah's prophecy of the suffering servant of God! The sufferings of Christ and His taking all our sins upon Himself in His death represent the very heart of the Gospel. We cannot have a Messiah without His suffering service on our behalf. The pathway leading to the eternal kingship of Jesus Christ passed through the valley of the shadow of death — the long shadow of the cross of Mt. Calvary. Christ's crown could only be worn by the crucified *Lamb of God, Who takes away the sin of the world!* (John 1:29b).

When we gather as the redeemed people of God to worship and to celebrate the Lord's Supper, we come as a people who were once mired in sin and unable to save ourselves. Yet we also come as a people whose iniquities and transgressions have been borne away from us by

Jesus Christ, our suffering servant, sent from God. Jesus' sufferings and death are represented before our eyes, minds, and hearts each and every time the Lord's Supper is set before us. Spiritually, we partake of Jesus body and blood, which He freely gave in exchange for our eternal forgiveness and acceptance in God our Father. Indeed, Christ surely has borne our griefs and carried our sorrows... and the Lord has laid upon Him the iniquity of us all!

PRAYER:

Gracious Lord, we thank You for revealing Christ's work and mission to Your prophet Isaiah more than seven hundred years before You brought Jesus, Your Messiah into this world to fulfill this prophecy. We especially thank and praise You that Jesus, Your Son, faithfully came, lived a perfect life, then suffered and died as our substitute, carrying our griefs and bearing our sorrows upon that cruel cross on Mt. Calvary.

We also praise You, Lord, for the way that You remind us of Jesus suffering service in saving us through the symbols of the bread and the cup of the Lord's Supper. By Your Spirit please empower us to remember more deeply and to rejoice ever more thankfully for Jesus and all that You have done for us through Him, both now, and for all eternity to come. In Jesus' name we pray. Amen.

38. He Shall Bear Their Iniquities

Yet it was the will of the Lord to crush him; he has put him to grief; when his soul makes an offering for guilt, he shall see his offspring; he shall prolong his days; the will of the Lord shall prosper in his hand.

Out of the anguish of his soul he shall see and be satisfied; by his knowledge shall the righteous one, my servant, make many to be accounted righteous, and he shall bear their iniquities.

Therefore I will divide him a portion with the many, and he shall divide the spoil with the strong, because he poured out his soul to death and was numbered with the transgressors; yet he bore the sin of many, and makes intercession for the transgressors.

Isaiah 53:10–12

PRINCIPLE:
Jesus Christ perfectly fulfilled the prophecies contained in Isaiah 52–53. It was the Lord Jesus who made an offering for our guilt. It was Christ Jesus who made many — all those who believe in His name — to be counted as righteous, all because of His own righteousness given to them. Although God's Son knew no sin and lived a perfect life, He nevertheless was counted among the transgressors and poured out His perfect soul unto death for our sakes.

And yet after bearing away our sins upon His shoulders, enduring separation from His Father, and after dying that cruel gruesome death on the cross, He rose again from the dead. As Isaiah foretold, *He shall prolong His days; the will of the Lord shall prosper in His hand.* And we know that Jesus in His triumph led a train of captives and gave gifts to men, for indeed He divided His victorious spoil with the many.

Every Lord's Supper celebrates Jesus' fulfillment of the great promise of Isaiah's prophecies concerning God's Messiah. As we partake of the elements in Communion we taste and we drink the symbols of Christ's suffering love for us. We come face to face spiritually with the Savior Who died so that we may live forevermore robed in His righteousness. And we understand that through Christ, the suffering servant, we have been delivered from the pollution and the judgment of our sin, in order to be adopted as sons and daughters of God. In Christ, we have received the many gifts, blessings, privileges gained for us among the spoils of His great triumph over sin, death, hell, and the devil.

> **PRAYER:**
>
> Lord Jesus, we thank You and praise You for willingly and faithfully laying aside the glories of the heavenly places and taking the form, not only of a servant, but of a suffering servant. We rejoice in the eternal power of Your absolute victory for our sakes through Your death on the cross in our place and by Your glorious resurrection from the dead. We exalt Your name as the King and Victor over all things, and we exalt the Father and the Holy Spirit, our faithful triune God. Please give us an even clearer vision of Your love for us as we remember, in the Supper, Your death and Your resurrection. In Your blessed name we pray. Amen.

39. A New Covenant in Jesus

> *"Behold, the days are coming, declares the Lord, when I will make a new covenant with the house of Israel and the house of Judah, not like the covenant that I made with their fathers on the day when I took them by the hand to bring them out of the land of Egypt, my covenant that they broke, though I was their husband, declares the Lord. For this is the covenant that I will make with the house of Israel after those days, declares the Lord: I will put my law within them, and I will write it on their hearts. And I will be their God, and they shall be my people. And no longer shall each one teach his neighbor and each his brother, saying, 'Know the Lord,' for they shall all know me, from the least of them to the greatest, declares the Lord. For I will forgive their iniquity, and I will remember their sin no more."*
>
> JEREMIAH 31:31–34

PRINCIPLE:

Many of the prophecies of Jeremiah have to do with announcing God's impending judgment on His people and calling upon them to repent from their many sins. However, in Jeremiah chapter 31, the Lord gives His prophet a revelation of great hope for the people of God in the future. That hope is a new covenant in which the Lord will put His *law within His people*, and He *will write it on their hearts*. This promised new covenant will enable all of God's people to know Him, *from the least of them to the greatest*.

The basis for this new covenant as it is revealed to Jeremiah is that the Lord *will forgive their iniquity and remember their sin no more*. And some six hundred years after it was announced, Jesus Christ purchased the forgiveness of our iniquities and ushered in God's new covenant. As the Holy Spirit was poured out after Jesus' ascension into heaven, He now makes His dwelling place in every believer and in doing so puts God's law within us, writing it upon our hearts.

We are today by faith the people of the new covenant sealed by the shed blood of Christ and its eternal benefits and blessings are applied to us by the Spirit of God, as He tabernacles within us. And so it is Jesus Christ we celebrate in the Lord's Supper, who has poured out His blood of the new covenant, and it is with the help of the Holy Spirit that we come and partake spiritually of the Son. The Sacrament is for us a new covenant meal, in which all the blessings of God's Covenant of Redemption are brought freshly to heart and to mind.

> **PRAYER:**
>
> Our gracious and loving heavenly Father, thank you for making a new covenant of salvation with us Your people through the work of Jesus Christ, Your Son. We give You honor and thanksgiving for Jesus' shed blood of this new covenant and for the many eternal blessings and benefits we receive by Your grace as the Holy Spirit works in us when we draw near to You in Communion. Please meet with us, Your new covenant people, as we receive the bread and the cup. And please send us from this Lord's Supper more equipped, energized, and empowered to share Your new covenant in Jesus with the many others who need to hear its Good News as well. In Jesus' name we pray. Amen.

40. I Will Put My Spirit Within You

> *Then he said to me, "Son of man, these bones are the whole house of Israel. Behold, they say, 'Our bones are dried up, and our hope is lost; we are indeed cut off.' Therefore prophesy, and say to them, Thus says the Lord God: Behold, I will open your graves and raise you from your graves, O my people. And I will bring you into the land of Israel. And you shall know that I am the Lord, when I open your graves, and raise you from your graves, O my people. And I will put my Spirit within you, and you shall live, and I will place you in your own land. Then you shall know that I am the Lord; I have spoken, and I will do it, declares the Lord."*
>
> EZEKIEL 37:11–14

PRINCIPLE:

Ezekiel's vision of the dry bones resurrected to newness of life is one of the most compelling images in the prophetic Scriptures. The Lord paints a vivid, unforgettable picture in Ezekiel 37 of what He intends to do for His people through Jesus Christ, His Son, and through the power of the Holy Spirit. Key to the resurrection of God's chosen people is His placing of His Spirit within us.

It is commonplace in many evangelical churches today to emphasize the work of the Father and of the Son in preaching, teaching, prayers, and praise. We rejoice in God the Father's plan to save a people for Himself from all the nations of the earth through His Covenant of Redemption. We praise and honor God the Son for His willing, grace-filled, service in order to fulfill His Father's plan. We marvel at the way Jesus took our sins upon Himself, accepted a condemnation He did nothing to deserve, died cruelly on that cross, and then rose again from that borrowed tomb in resurrection glory.

But what of the Holy Spirit's amazing work in our redemption to eternal life? When Jesus ascended into heaven, He and His Father sent forth the Holy Spirit, just as He had promised His disciples. The Holy Spirit was poured out on all who were chosen in Christ. The Holy Spirit, the third Person of the Trinity, applied all the benefits and blessings of what Christ had accomplished to man, woman, and child in which He had taken up His residence. And the Holy Spirit continues in doing this astounding work in every believer up to this very hour.

The one true eternal Spirit of the living God condescends to take up His residence within every person whom God had chosen and who calls on the name of the Lord. If you are a believer in Christ as you read this devotion, then you have the very holy presence of God living within you! It is truly an amazing work which God has done in us through His Spirit in applying Christ's redemption to each one who believes.

It is also by the Holy Spirit that we come to the celebration of the Lord's Supper. The Spirit uses the simple elements of bread and the cup, along with the words of institution, in order to remind us of what Jesus Christ did to give us newness of life. And the Spirit of Christ also conveys to us God's spiritual grace and strengthening power as we come and partake of the Sacrament by faith, truly discerning the body of Christ.

PRAYER:
O gracious heavenly Father, help us to draw near to Your Sacrament through the ministry of Your Holy Spirit. Cause us to receive the bread and the cup with truly grateful hearts for all that Jesus Your Son has done to redeem us from the pit of death and to breathe into us newness of life — resurrection life! May we get up from Your Supper refreshed, renewed, and reminded by Your Spirit. And may we more fully worship and adore the Holy Spirit, even as we do You, our Father, and the blessed Son. In Whose name we pray. Amen.

41. I Will Be Their God

> *They shall not defile themselves anymore with their idols and their detestable things, or with any of their transgressions. But I will save them from all the backslidings in which they have sinned, and will cleanse them; and they shall be my people, and I will be their God.*
>
> EZEKIEL 37:23

PRINCIPLE:

Ezekiel 37:23 sometimes gets overlooked in this famous chapter of Scripture, as it comes near the end of the verses after Ezekiel's vision of the dry bones brought back to life. And yet this verse foretells what God would later do for all His people through Jesus Christ, His Messiah and our Savior.

The Lord describes in this passage a time in which He would gather all of His people from among the nations and make of them one faithful nation, ruled by one Davidic king, living under an everlasting covenant of peace. Ezekiel received this revelation in the times when both the kingdom of Israel and the kingdom of Judah had been cast into exile; the northern tribes into the Assyrian Empire and the people of Judah into the Neo-Babylonian Empire. And thus this prophecy served to give God's people great hope for a brighter future under the blessings of their sovereign Lord.

There is a sense in which this promise has three stages of fulfillment. The first one of these stages occurred beginning in 539 BC, as the Persian king Cyrus permitted the exiles' resettlement in the land of their forefathers and helped fund the rebuilding of the temple in Jerusalem. The second and much fuller stage of fulfillment was inaugurated when God's Son Jesus Christ came to His people, and in their refusal to receive Him, He was crucified, dead, and buried. With His wondrous resurrection from the dead and His pouring out of the Holy Spirit on all who believe, He began building a kingdom of people purchased by His blood, making one covenantal nation *from every tribe and language and people and nation* (Revelation 5:9–10). We continue to live today in the second stage of the fulfillment of Ezekiel 37:23. The third and last stage of fulfillment will occur when Jesus Christ returns in glory to this earth, executes the Day of Judgment, and creates a new heaven and new earth — one holy nation of redeemed and resurrected people of God, without sin or sorrow or pain or death, living and rejoicing in God's presence forever more, constantly giving glory to Jesus the Lamb of God who reigns as King of kings and Lord of lords.

Part of the celebrations which will take place with this final stage of fulfillment will be the marriage supper of the Lamb. And all those who believe in the name of Jesus and whose names are written in the Lamb's book of life will be invited to this great feast as King Jesus is joined for all eternity future with His perfectly prepared Bride, His Church of the redeemed and elect of God. Every Lord's Supper observance is a foretaste of this coming celebration in glory.

PRAYER:

Dear Lord, we pray that you will build in us through the Lord's Supper, a sweet anticipation of Your return in glory and the final fulfillment of the revelation You gave so long ago to Your servant Ezekiel. May we have a holy longing to see You in the fullness of Your glory and majesty, even as we see You distantly, by faith, and through the symbols of Your incarnation, death, and resurrection — in the bread and the cup. May You be exalted and glorified as the Holy Spirit draws us together around Your family table. In Jesus' name we pray. Amen.

42. Jesus' Everlasting Dominion

> *"I saw in the night visions, and behold, with the clouds of heaven there came one like a son of man, and he came to the Ancient of Days and was presented before him.*
>
> *And to him was given dominion and glory and a kingdom, that all peoples, nations, and languages should serve him; his dominion is an everlasting dominion, which shall not pass away, and his kingdom one that shall not be destroyed.*
>
> DANIEL 7:13–14

PRINCIPLE:

While Daniel was serving the Lord in the great civil administrations of the Neo-Babylonian and Persian Empires, he also fulfilled the role of a prophet and dream interpreter of God. One of the most glorious visions Daniel received is recorded in Daniel, chapter 7. What is particularly compelling about this portion of the larger vision is the arrival of *one like the son of man*, a person of glorified yet human appearance, who receives an everlasting, unconquerable kingdom.

The Lord Jesus most often referred to Himself as the Son of Man during His earthy ministry, and later, in the great vision of Revelation chapter 5, John is shown the same glorious vision in which Jesus, the Lamb who was slain yet who lives, receives this everlasting dominion, composed of people from every tribe, and nation, and language (Revelation 5:9–10). Thus we now know, as those who live in light of what Jesus has accomplished and what Jesus has received from His Father, that Daniel was shown the great enthronement of King Jesus at His ascension into the heavens after His resurrection from the dead.

We also understand that as believers in King Jesus we are also citizens of His everlasting dominion. We are in fact vice-regents, who are called to sit beside the Lord on His throne and judge the nations. We are redeemed in order to be *a kingdom and priests to our God and we shall reign upon the earth* (Revelation 5:10). Our citizenship is ultimately in the kingdom of Christ and our passports are stamped with the phrase, *holy to the Lord*.

And so as we come to the Lord's Supper we come as a community of citizens in the everlasting kingdom of God, ruled over by the King of kings and Lord of lords, Jesus Christ the Son. For us the Lord's Supper is the King's lavish banquet table and we are invited to draw near and to eat and to drink of the spiritual grace of God to the full.

King Jesus encourages us to come to His feast and to rejoice in Him and in the salvation that He has purchased for us. And in the Lord's Supper we see by faith, dimly yet truly, the reflection of the sparkling delights which await us in eternity future as adopted children of the King.

> **PRAYER:**
> Our gracious and loving heavenly Father, please use this celebration of the Lord's Supper to reveal to us even more of the glorious kingly presence of Jesus Christ our Savior. Help us to grasp the incredible blessing that we come to Your table as redeemed children of the King. Empower us to eat and drink deeply from Your eternal, abounding grace. Cause us to embrace our citizenship in Your unconquerable kingdom. Transform us more fully into image bearers of King Jesus. And it is in Jesus' mighty name we pray. Amen.

43. I Will Rejoice in the Lord

> *Though the fig tree should not blossom, nor fruit be on the vines, the produce of the olive fail and the fields yield no food, the flock be cut off from the fold and there be no herd in the stalls, yet I will rejoice in the Lord; I will take joy in the God of my salvation. God, the Lord, is my strength; he makes my feet like the deer's; he makes me tread on my high places.*
>
> HABAKKUK 3:17–19

PRINCIPLE:
God's people were facing difficult times in the late seventh century B.C. when Habakkuk served as a prophet. The northern kingdom had already been obliterated and its people carried into Assyrian exile. The fearsome Assyrians had also threatened the southern kingdom of Judah and now another super power was on the rise — the Neo-Babylonian Empire. The Lord was now judging His own people's idolatry and disobedience using the cruel instruments of the surrounding pagan nations.

In the first portion of Habakkuk's book, he complains and questions God about the state of His people and the rampant violence of that age. Yet, like Job many years before, Habakkuk is later inspired by God's Spirit to find his peace and his joy in the God of his salvation. The Lord causes him to see that despite the unfruitful and unproductive appearance of immediate circumstances, He remains with His servant and with His people. Habakkuk was empowered to see beyond the outward appearances of things and to behold the faithfulness of God using the spiritual eyes of faith.

All of us experience times of great difficulty and trial in our lives. And when those times come, we are very tempted to view God and our relationship with Him through the outward appearances of trying times. We can doubt the Lord's goodness and our place in His kingdom family. We can also, like Habakkuk, question the way that God is dealing with us or with other believers around us. And yet, if we draw near to God in such times rather than pulling away from Him — if we by grace and faith can gaze past the outward appearance and into the true character of the God of our salvation — then like Habakkuk we can rejoice in the Lord and sing His many praises.

Sometimes it is difficult to come to the Lord's Supper when we are facing severe afflictions or conflict in our lives. We are so preoccupied with our sufferings and our doubts and questions concerning God's faithfulness that we fail to see the point at all in participating in the Sacrament. And yet the Lord Jesus Christ encourages us to come to His table in order to remember — to remember the greatest sacrifice of love and compassion which has ever been given. As we receive the bread and the cup the Spirit of Christ reminds us of Jesus' love for us and of the eternal joy we have in His salvation. Through the Supper we are also strengthened according to His grace. We learn not to judge God, or His love for us, or the status of our relationship with Him, based upon our immediate trials, but instead to see God through the loving sacrifice of Christ Jesus, His Son, our Lord and Savior.

PRAYER:
Heavenly Father and God of our salvation, we thank You that You will never leave us or forsake us. We praise You that You abide with us at all times, whether times of ease and blessings or times of hardness and lacking. Strengthen us in perilous times, gracious and powerful Father. And increase within us joyfulness and gratitude for Jesus Christ, Your Son, and for the fellowship we have with You through the comforting presence of the Holy Spirit. We pray this in Jesus' name. Amen.

Gospel Feasting

New Testament Lord's Supper Devotions

44. Hosanna in the Highest!

> *Now when they drew near to Jerusalem and came to Bethphage, to the Mount of Olives, then Jesus sent two disciples, saying to them, "Go into the village in front of you, and immediately you will find a donkey tied, and a colt with her. Untie them and bring them to me. If anyone says anything to you, you shall say, 'The Lord needs them,' and he will send them at once." This took place to fulfill what was spoken by the prophet, saying,*
>
> > *"Say to the daughter of Zion,*
> > *'Behold, your king is coming to you,*
> > *humble, and mounted on a donkey,*
> > *and on a colt, the foal of a beast of burden.'"*
>
> *The disciples went and did as Jesus had directed them. They brought the donkey and the colt and put on them their cloaks, and he sat on them. Most of the crowd spread their cloaks on the road, and others cut branches from the trees and spread them on the road. And the crowds that went before him and that followed him were shouting, "Hosanna to the Son of David! Blessed is he who comes in the name of the Lord! Hosanna in the highest!" And when he entered Jerusalem, the whole city was stirred up, saying, "Who is this?" And the crowds said, "This is the prophet Jesus, from Nazareth of Galilee."*
>
> MATTHEW 21:1–11

PRINCIPLE:

Surely one of the most marvelous scenes that unfolded during the lifetime of the Lord Jesus was the triumphal entry into Jerusalem we celebrate every year on Palm Sunday. To anyone observing the events that day, who knew their Jewish prophets, this was the long-expected exaltation of the anointed servant of God, the promised Messiah. Here now finally, or so it appeared that day, the nation of Israel was joyfully receiving their deliverer and hailing Him as their rightful King.

Interestingly, even the cry "Hosanna," shouted by the exultant crowds lining Jesus' humble procession would seem to indicate that the people knew who Christ was. The term means, *save now*, or *pray save us*. They were referring to Jesus as a Savior of His people. And at the end of Matthew's account of these events, indeed crowds identified Him as *the prophet Jesus, from Nazareth of Galilee*.

Of course, the Bible records that another crowd of Jewish people would later cry out for Jesus' crucifixion near the end of that eventful week. And it was on the night, just hours before His betrayal to be crucified, that Jesus established the Lord's Supper as a means of remembering what the Son of David was about to do, serving as the Savior of His people from their sins.

> **PRAYER:**
>
> Heavenly Father, we praise You not only for Jesus' triumphal entry into Jerusalem in fulfillment of Zechariah's prophecy, but even more so for Jesus' triumph on the cross over sin, death, hell, and Satan. And we praise Jesus for declaring the new Passover as He prepared to die for our sins by commanding us to celebrate perpetually the Lord's Supper, a feast of salvation, of remembrance, and of anticipation. As we celebrate the Supper together, help us by Your Spirit to remember the events of Jesus' ministry during that final week for all of us who believe in His name. Amen.

45. Merciful

"When the Son of Man comes in his glory, and all the angels with him, then he will sit on his glorious throne. Before him will be gathered all the nations, and he will separate people one from another as a shepherd separates the sheep from the goats. And he will place the sheep on his right, but the goats on the left. Then the King will say to those on his right, 'Come, you who are blessed by my Father, inherit the kingdom prepared for you from the foundation of the world. For I was hungry and you gave me food, I was thirsty and you gave me drink, I was a stranger and you welcomed me, I was naked and you clothed me, I was sick and you visited me, I was in prison and you came to me.' Then the righteous will answer him, saying, 'Lord, when did we see you hungry and feed you, or thirsty and give you drink? And when did we see you a stranger and welcome you, or naked and clothe you? And when did we see you sick or in prison and visit you?' And the King will answer them, 'Truly, I say to you, as you did it to one of the least of these my brothers, you did it to me.'

MATTHEW 25:31–40

PRINCIPLE:

The theme of Matthew 25:31–40 is of the importance of showing true mercy to others in need — mercy given solely because of the mercy first given to us by the Lord Jesus Christ. The Lord's mercy is far more immense than meeting our simple physical needs in this life. Nevertheless, the Lord, while ministering prior to His death on the cross, often depicted His majestic eternal mercies through acts of physical healing and the meeting of physical needs.

As believers in the Lord Jesus Christ, His ambassadors, and His fellow heirs, we too are called to show forth the great mercies of God our Father in Christ through simple acts of compassion and assistance to those in need. This truth is explicitly declared in the passage above from the Gospel of Matthew.

Our status as *sheep,* rather than *goats* on the last day will depend upon the choosing of God and the faith He has mercifully given to us in Christ Jesus. Yet if we truly do stand in God's sight as His adopted son or daughter, then our faith will show forth the fruits of a redeemed, transformed heart. This means that the eternal grace we have received in God's loving mercy will be reflected in the mercy we truly show to others.

The Lord's Supper is for us a physical reminder — a visual and tactile demonstration — representing for us the eternal grace, mercy, and provision we have received from God our Father through the Lord Jesus Christ and the indwelling Holy Spirit. May the Spirit of Christ display in us, through our participation in the Supper, the abundant and eternal provision of God in meeting our deepest needs. And may the Lord use our Communion celebrations to move us to display outwardly, physically, and tangibly before others in need the amazing, abundant, and transforming provisions of mercy, springing from Christ alone!

> **PRAYER:**
> O Lord our God, we praise You, and Your Son our Savior, and the Holy Spirit. We thank You for Your abundant grace and provision for us. We thank You for Your eternal compassion embodied in Jesus' saving death on the cross and His pouring out of the Holy Spirit on us to help us and sustain us in this life. Holy Father, may we also be gracious and compassionate toward others in need, both physically and spiritually. And may we provide for them, using our resources and also seeking those resources which can only be supplied as we come to You. In Jesus' name we pray. Amen.

46. He Is Risen, He Is Risen Indeed!

> *Now after the Sabbath, toward the dawn of the first day of the week, Mary Magdalene and the other Mary went to see the tomb. And behold, there was a great earthquake, for an angel of the Lord descended from heaven and came and rolled back the stone and sat on it. His appearance was like lightning, and his clothing white as snow. And for fear of him the guards trembled and became like dead men. But the angel said to the women, "Do not be afraid, for I know that you seek Jesus who was crucified. He is not here, for he has risen, as he said. Come, see the place where he lay. Then go quickly and tell his disciples that he has risen from the dead, and behold, he is going before you to Galilee; there you will see him. See, I have told you." So they departed quickly from the tomb with fear and great joy, and ran to tell his disciples. And behold, Jesus met them and said, "Greetings!" And they came up and took hold of his feet and worshiped him. Then Jesus said to them, "Do not be afraid; go and tell my brothers to go to Galilee, and there they will see me."*
>
> MATTHEW 28:1–10

PRINCIPLE:
Every day we celebrate the glorious resurrection of the Lord Jesus Christ! Our joy in Christ's victory is not limited to one Sabbath per year. The event described here in Matthew 28, and in the other Gospels, is the defining event of all of redemptive history, for early on that first day of the week just outside the walls of Jerusalem, sin, death, hell, and the devil were defeated by the victory of Jesus! The Lord's one-time substitutionary sacrifice was accepted by God the Father and proved in His Son's rising from the dead.

As we celebrate this amazing event, we glory not only in the fact that Jesus conquered sin and death, but also in the fact that we are united together with Him by the Holy Spirit in faith. We also are more than conquerors through Him who loved us so very much! In Christ, we walk in newness of life and one day will also live eternally in resurrection glory just as the Lord Jesus does at this very moment.

In our coming to the Lord's Supper, let us ask the Lord's Spirit to remind us of the blessed hope we profess in Jesus. Our blessed hope is that just as He rose from the dead and now lives forevermore in a glorified state — so one day we will also, as those found in Him by faith. The token of this promise that Jesus has given us is this fellowship meal called the Lord's Supper, or Communion. Symbolized in our present and real spiritual fellowship with the Lord Jesus is our ultimate, one day coming, future fuller fellowship with Him and all the glorified saints in life at the celebration of the great marriage supper of the Lamb!

Let us glory in the completed work of the Lord Jesus Christ in offering Himself once for all, for everyone who trusts in Him by faith. Let us raise our voices in praise and thanksgiving. And let us revel in the revelation of His resurrection and in His present fellowship with us by His Spirit. Let us also rejoice in our future expectation of His eternal immediate presence with us, represented in the Sacrament of the Lord's Supper.

Christ Is Risen! Christ Is Risen Indeed!

PRAYER:
Heavenly Father, we praise You and honor You and adore You for the miraculous way You purchased our eternal salvation through Jesus Christ, Your Son, our Lord. We thank you that You did not leave the Lord Jesus sealed in that borrowed tomb, but raised Him victoriously from the dead! We thank You that we have the certain promise from You that just as You raised the Lord Jesus by the power of the Spirit from the dead and clothed Him in resurrection glory, so also You will do the same for us one day at His appearing. Help us as we celebrate Communion together to remember that day of Jesus' resurrection victory and also to be renewed in the joy of our blessed hope — that at Jesus' glorious return, we too will be raised from the dead and clothed in resurrection glory. In the risen Lord Jesus' name. Amen.

47. Kingdom Commission

> *And Jesus came and said to them, "All authority in heaven and on earth has been given to me. Go therefore and make disciples of all nations, baptizing them in the name of the Father and of the Son and of the Holy Spirit, teaching them to observe all that I have commanded you. And behold, I am with you always, to the end of the age."*
>
> MATTHEW 28:18–20

PRINCIPLE:

There are several interesting connections between the Great Commission, which the Lord Jesus Christ gave to us as His Church, and His institution of the Supper. Ever since the earliest days of the church, the distinguishing mark of someone who had been made a disciple of Jesus was his admission to the Lord's Table. In the ancient church, those who had not professed Christ and been baptized and received into visible membership were actually sent away during the worship service at the time just prior to the congregational celebration of Communion. Indeed, one of the most anticipated events in the life of a new believer in those days was his or her first opportunity to receive the Sacrament. As each new disciple was made, in fulfillment of Christ's Great Commission, the occasion was marked by the Lord's Supper.

Communion also operates, as a means of God's grace, in building up believers in their faith and practice, thus serving as a helper in the process of discipling. The importance of this was not lost on the early churches, as they typically broke bread together on a weekly basis in commemoration of the Lord's Last Supper with His disciples. The elders of the church saw it as part of their responsibility in carrying out the Great Commission to see to it that their flocks were fully nourished on the richness of God's grace provided by the preaching of the Word, prayer, and the celebration around the Lord's Table. In doing this, the pastors and other elders were simply doing as Christ directed, *teaching them to observe all that I have commanded you.* The Lord specifically directed the disciples to eat of the bread and drink of the cup in remembrance of Him. And of course the Apostle Paul was told by the Lord Jesus that whenever the Lord's Supper was celebrated, the believers *proclaimed the Lord's death until He comes* (1 Corinthians 11:26).

Finally, the Lord's Supper also communicates to us the reality of the kingdom age in which we now live as believers in Christ. For, just as the Lord Jesus promised the disciples in Matthew 28:20, *I am with you always, to the end of the age,* so it is with the Lord's Supper. For each and every time believers celebrate the Supper, the Lord Jesus is truly present — not physically — but spiritually, through the powerful and gracious operation of His Holy Spirit. Christ's presence with us is continual in this way while He builds His kingdom here on the earth, right up until the day of His return and the end of this age. Yet, His presence with us on that will not end. Instead it will become all the more intense and immediate, as we celebrate the marriage supper of the Lamb and abide with Him forevermore!

PRAYER:
Our gracious and loving heavenly Father, we praise You for the way that You are building Your kingdom on this earth under the victorious reign of the Lord Jesus Christ. We praise You for giving to us Your Great Commission, calling us to go and as we go to make disciples for You from all the nations. We praise You and thank You for giving us the Lord's Supper as an observance of grace, remembrance, and encouragement to keep, until the Lord Jesus returns in the fullness of His glory. In Jesus' name. Amen.

48. The King, the Kingdom of God, and the Supper

And he said to them, "This is my blood of the covenant, which is poured out for many. Truly, I say to you, I will not drink again of the fruit of the vine until that day when I drink it new in the kingdom of God."

MARK 14:24–25

And when the hour came, he reclined at the table, and the apostles with him. And he said to them, "I have earnestly desired to eat this Passover with you before I suffer. For I tell you I will not eat it until it is fulfilled in the kingdom of God."

LUKE 22:14–16

PRINCIPLE:
It is important for us to realize that Jesus preached and taught the kingdom of God as both present *and* future. From the very beginning of Jesus' ministry, He declared the kingdom's nearness, as in Mark 1:15: *The time is fulfilled, and the kingdom of God is at hand; repent and believe the gospel.* We understand that Jesus inaugurated His Father's kingdom during His lifetime and that the kingdom has been growing and developing ever since.

But there is also a future focus in Jesus' kingdom proclamations, such as His words to the disciples during His last Passover meal with them on the night He was betrayed. Based upon our Lord's statements to the disciples during that Last Supper, there is a "not-yet-ness" aspect of the kingdom of God that awaits its final consummation (or fulfillment) when Jesus returns in glory.

As we gather around the Lord's Table and remember the inauguration of the kingdom in Jesus' incarnation, life, suffering, death, and resurrection, we also anticipate the second coming of Christ, when the kingdom will be fully realized. At that time, Jesus our King and Savior will drink of the fruit of the vine with us *new in the kingdom of God.* Everyone who has been redeemed by the blood of Christ through the gift of faith will be invited to sit at the marriage supper of the Lamb. May our Communion celebration be for us a foretaste of that perpetual, worshipful feast unto God and to the Lamb. May our Lord's Supper observances always be visual proclamations of the kingdom of God and of the Gospel of Jesus Christ.

> **PRAYER:**
> Heavenly Father, we thank You that the struggles and trials of this present world — the constant battle between Your disciples and the enemies of Your kingdom — will one day cease. We thank You that there is a certain day of absolute victory and triumph when the Lord Jesus will return and the new heaven and new earth will be established forevermore. Dear Lord, until that bright and glorious day arrives, help us by Your Spirit to keep the Gospel feast that You have appointed, the Lord's Supper. And cause us to celebrate this kingdom feast as those who eagerly await the return of King Jesus, that we may celebrate His absolute victory with Him in the wonders of the marriage supper of the Lamb. In Jesus' name. Amen.

49. Strength with His Arm

> *And his mercy is for those who fear him from generation to generation. He has shown strength with his arm; he has scattered the proud in the thoughts of their hearts; he has brought down the mighty from their thrones and exalted those of humble estate; he has filled the hungry with good things, and the rich he has sent away empty. He has helped his servant Israel, in remembrance of his mercy, as he spoke to our fathers, to Abraham and to his offspring forever.*
>
> Luke 1:50–55

PRINCIPLE:
Our primary focus during our annual Christmastime is certainly and properly God's gift of His Son, our Savior. The Lord Jesus embodies the wondrousness of God's abundant provision, emphasized in the texts we usually choose for worship and for reflection. The text above is from a portion known as the Magnificat, Mary's exaltation of the God of our salvation and His marvelous means of bringing it to fruition.

This is a wonderful portion of the Gospel of Luke for us to use as we prepare to approach the Lord's Table. Notice how Mary is inspired to rejoice in the Lord's grace toward His people. While she begins her praise concerning what God has brought about specifically for her, she quickly is carried along by the Spirit's work to declare the praises of God's mercy and His provision for all God's elect — from generation to generation — to Abraham and to his offspring forever.

Through the child, promised and fulfilled, the mighty of the world have indeed been brought low, while those of humble estate have by faith been exalted. Those of the people of God hungry to be filled with the Word of God and with His righteousness have been given all the good things of Christ Jesus through the Holy Spirit. All of this brought about by the strength of His arm — that One who did not consider *equality with the Father a thing to be grasped, but made Himself nothing, taking the form of a servant* (Philippians 2:6–7). The divine servant, the Lord Jesus Christ, indeed helped the servants of God, accomplishing their deliverance when He came into this world, lived a perfect life, suffered and died, and then rose again — so that we who believe have everlasting life!

The portions of bread and fruit of the vine we receive during Communion are rather small. In purely physical terms they can do little to satisfy our hunger for nourishment and for good things. Yet, they serve to symbolically represent, and by the powerful working of the Holy Spirit, they do indeed provide immense, eternal, good things of God, for the nourishment of our souls, abounding to our growth in grace. Our daily food must be the Word of the living God, and like Jesus, to do the will of the One who sent Him and through Him saved us. As we come to the Lord's Supper, let us rejoice in the God of our salvation, through Jesus Christ, the Word made flesh — the One who is both Son of God and Son of Man!

PRAYER:
Heavenly Father, we rejoice that You are truly the God of our eternal salvation! We praise You for the Lord Jesus Christ, Your mighty arm of power Who has worked Your salvation for everyone who believes in Your great name. Gracious and omnipotent Father, we ask You to feed us spiritually upon Your amazing and sustaining grace as we partake together in the Lord's Supper. Encourage us. Equip us. And energize us for sharing the Gospel of Jesus with our families, our friends, our neighbors, our co-workers, our fellow students, and anyone You choose to place along our pathway in this present life of faith. In Jesus' mighty name. Amen.

50. Your Salvation

> *And he came in the Spirit into the temple, and when the parents brought in the child Jesus, to do for him according to the custom of the Law, he took him up in his arms and blessed God and said, "Lord, now you are letting your servant depart in peace, according to your word; for my eyes have seen your salvation that you have prepared in the presence of all peoples, a light for revelation to the Gentiles, and for glory to your people Israel."*
>
> LUKE 2:27–32

PRINCIPLE:

Another aspect of our celebration of the incarnation and birth of the Lord Jesus Christ, is discovered by looking at the prophesy of Simeon recorded in Luke chapter 2. The Spirit of God came upon Simeon and promised him that he would not be gathered to his fathers until he had seen the Christ — the promised Messiah of God. The wonderful man of God encountered Joseph and Mary as they brought the infant Jesus to the temple courts in Jerusalem in order to observe all that was commanded for firstborns.

Simeon's inspired words convey very simply, yet very powerfully, the redemptive task the divine Son had been sent by God the Father to do among His people. Jesus came into the world of men and embodied in His person and work the salvation of God! The holy and righteous God determined before all time with His Son to offer Him up as a sacrifice in our place, bearing the fierce wrath of God and removing the stain of our sins.

Simeon also seemed to understand that the Lord Jesus came not for God's outwardly identified people, the nation of Israel, but for all those inwardly identified, Jew and Gentile, whom the Lord was pleased to call. This is also crucial to the Good News of Jesus — the truth that God has purchased for Himself, through the blood of the Lamb, a people from every tribe and language and people and nation. In doing so, He declares His people a kingdom and priests (Revelation 5:9–10).

We who believe in the Lord Jesus Christ by faith alone for salvation have also seen the salvation of our God, a salvation He has *prepared in the presence of all peoples, a light for revelation to the Gentiles and for glory to Your people Israel*. As we come to the Lord's Supper today, we partake by faith in the salvation and sanctification God has prepared in the presence of all peoples, through the Lord Jesus

Christ and the work of the Holy Spirit. May we be enabled by the Spirit of Christ today to see with transformed spiritual eyes, mind, and heart, the mighty and eternal salvation of our God!

> **PRAYER:**
>
> Heavenly Father, may the salvation that You have prepared for all the nations of people in Your Son Jesus Christ be proclaimed clearly in our services of worship, first from our pulpit and then in our celebrations of the Lord's Supper. By the power of Your Spirit and according to the faith You have given to us in Christ, may we ever and always lift high the sacrifice of Jesus for our eternal salvation and for all those who will believe in Your name. May our Communion feasts proclaim the Gospel in visual and symbolic ways which reinforce the Good News preached from the pulpit. And may our unity as the body of Christ around the Table be a testimony that Your salvation has also been prepared and applied to us, who are now spiritually the children of Abraham and heirs of Your promise to him. We ask this in Jesus' name. Amen.

51. The Gracious, Forgiving Father and the Supper

I will arise and go to my father, and I will say to him, "Father, I have sinned against heaven and before you. I am no longer worthy to be called your son. Treat me as one of your hired servants. And he arose and came to his father. But while he was still a long way off, his father saw him and felt compassion, and ran and embraced him and kissed him. And the son said to him, 'Father, I have sinned against heaven and before you. I am no longer worthy to be called your son.' But the father said to his servants, 'Bring quickly the best robe, and put it on him, and put a ring on his hand, and shoes on his feet. And bring the fattened calf and kill it, and let us eat and celebrate. For this my son was dead, and is alive again; he was lost, and is found.' And they began to celebrate.

LUKE 15:18−24

PRINCIPLE:
Jesus told the Parable of the Prodigal Son as an illustration for principles of His kingdom. This portion of the parable teaches us of the abundant grace, forgiveness, and compassion God our Father showers upon His wayward children when they are redeemed by faith in the Lord. The prodigal son's regret and repentance described in such poignant language by Jesus reminds us of our own Spirit-birthed conviction and turning to God in Christ. In many ways like this wayward child, we come before God painfully aware that we *have sinned against heaven and before Him*, and are unworthy in every respect.

But as we turn to our Father in true faith through Jesus, we find that He has already come and embraced us in His eternal love and compassion. Through the imputation, or crediting of Christ's righteousness to us, when God looks upon us He sees His one and only beloved Son — for we are adopted in Jesus. All of those markers of identity in God's family are sealed into us by His Spirit, much as the robe, the ring, and shoes are given to the returning son in the parable.

But the father's joy over his son's return did not end with his loving embrace, or with the bestowal of the outward signs of his 'readoption' into the family. The Father's joy was so abundant and exuberant that he wanted to share that joy with his family, his friends, and all the village. And so he ordered a great celebration — a feast with the finest of food and music and dancing. As he later tells his older son in the story, *It was fitting to celebrate and be glad, for this your brother was dead, and is alive; he was lost, and is found.*

Let us gather around the Lord's Table as those who are celebrating a great feast — a joyous event for each and all of us as those who were once dead in trespasses and sins, who have been made alive together in Jesus Christ; as those who once were lost — strangers and aliens from God, who have been found and declared to be sons and daughters of our heavenly Father.

PRAYER:
Our gracious and loving heavenly Father, we thank You and praise You that, although we stubbornly went our own prodigal way, You gave us Your Spirit and brought us to our senses according to faith in Jesus. We thank You for drawing us away from the pigsty which was our former way of life and back into the joys of Your eternal embrace. Thank You for receiving us with joyfulness and celebration. Thank You for preparing this Gospel Feast of the Lord's Supper so that we can receive Your grace and provision and so that we can offer You our praise and adoration. In Jesus' name. Amen.

52. Recognizing Jesus in the Supper

> *So they drew near to the village to which they were going. He acted as if he were going farther, but they urged him strongly, saying, "Stay with us, for it is toward evening and the day is now far spent." So he went in to stay with them. When he was at table with them, he took the bread and blessed and broke it and gave it to them. And their eyes were opened, and they recognized him. And he vanished from their sight. They said to each other, "Did not our hearts burn within us while he talked to us on the road, while he opened to us the Scriptures?"*
>
> LUKE 24:28–32

PRINCIPLE:

On the day of Jesus' resurrection there were two followers of Christ traveling down a road from Jerusalem to the village of Emmaus. As they engaged in a lively conversation about the things they had seen and heard in Jerusalem during the previous seven days, another man came alongside them and joined in their discussion. When these two disciples of Jesus expressed their amazement that some of the disciples and some of the women had found Jesus' tomb empty, the stranger said to them, *O foolish ones, and slow of heart to believe all that the prophets have spoken! Was it not necessary that the Christ should suffer these things and enter into his glory?* (Luke 24:25–26). And he continued with them, interpreting for them all that was written in the Scriptures concerning the Messiah.

All this time the two men had no idea who this fellow traveler was, for they were kept from recognizing him. It was only at the moment when they sat down to break bread with him that their eyes were opened and they realized that the one who had shared the road with them was in fact the risen Christ!

When we gather together for worship each Lord's Day, we have the revealed Word of God — the Scriptures — opened to us by faithful preaching. The Holy Spirit makes this effective, applying the Word to our hearts. When this is joined with the celebration of the Lord's bread and cup around the Communion table, we are enabled to receive a heightened recognition of the risen, resurrected, and reigning Lord Jesus. As we come to the Lord's Supper, in joyful praise to God for the resurrection of Jesus, let us ask our Father to open our eyes anew — to sharpen our spiritual vision — in order that we may recognize the spiritual presence of our risen Savior and King at table with us!

> **PRAYER:**
>
> Dear Lord our Redeemer, please reveal Yourself to us as we celebrate the Supper. Open our eyes to see You more fully through the working of the Holy Spirit. As the bread of Communion is blessed and broken, may we come to understand Your special presence among Your people gathered for worship and the Sacrament. As You do this within us, may we long to behold You fully, face to face, as You have promised we will indeed be able to do when You return and we celebrate the marriage supper of the Lamb. In Your holy name we pray. Amen.

53. Jesus the Revealer of God and the Supper

> *In the beginning was the Word, and the Word was with God, and the Word was God. He was in the beginning with God.... And the Word became flesh and dwelt among us, and we have seen his glory, glory as of the only Son from the Father, full of grace and truth.... And from his fullness we have all received, grace upon grace. For the law was given through Moses; grace and truth came through Jesus Christ. No one has ever seen God; the only God, who is at the Father's side, he has made him known.*
> JOHN 1:1–2, 14, 16–18

PRINCIPLE:

The Apostle John introduces us to the Gospel of Jesus Christ using words and phrases that deliberately remind us of God's amazing work of creation as revealed in the first verses of Genesis. John confidently declares to us that Jesus the Son — *the Word* — was with God the Father at the beginning of all things. In fact, the Apostle goes further in identifying Jesus as fully God.

We understand with the help of other Scriptures from the Bible, that what John is getting at when he speaks of Jesus as the Word in the beginning with God, is that he is communicating to us that Jesus the Son is eternal and was both present and actively involved in the creation of all things. Paul writes of this in Colossians 1:16:

> *For by him all things were created, in heaven and on earth, visible and invisible, whether thrones of dominions or rulers or authorities — all things were created through him and for him.*

And yet John's introduction of Jesus Christ to us also declares His incarnation: *And the Word became flesh and dwelt among us...* The same divine Son who spoke light and sky and sea and life into being came to dwell among men — came to live and breathe in human flesh within His creation. He is the true light and source of life.

Now while John will indeed go on within the chapters of his Gospel to explain Jesus' incarnation in light of His suffering and death in our place as the *Lamb of God who takes away the sin of the world* (John 1:29b). These earliest verses declare another purpose for Jesus' incarnation — He serves as the ultimate revelation of God!

John writes that as they beheld Jesus, they saw His glory, *glory as of the only Son from the Father, full of grace and truth.* Jesus came to reveal the glory, the grace, and the truth of God to His people. John describes Christ as the giver of grace upon grace, to those who believe. He also declares Him to be the only means by which we can know God the Father.

As we gather together around the Lord's Table today, let us prayerfully seek the Spirit of Christ to enable us to spiritually see and to know more fully the glorious revelation of God our Father through Jesus Christ His Son. May the Holy Spirit quicken our remembrance and our faith concerning Jesus' incarnation, His life, and His atoning death for our eternal sakes. May we behold with spiritual eyes the risen, ascended, and reigning King Jesus — presently seated with the Father in glory. May we find in Him our sure and certain hope of the resurrection and the marriage supper of the Lamb. And let us ever and always look to this glorious Son, who brings to us the fullness of grace and truth, by the Spirit of God.

PRAYER:

Heavenly Father, by the power of Your Spirit please give to us grace upon grace through Jesus Christ our Lord as we partake of this Sacrament. Please help us to know You through the gloriousness and the grace and truth of Your Son Jesus. There are so many religions, popular movements, and famous individuals telling us that we can find our way to You on many different paths. Help us to ever have in our hearts and minds this revelation that Jesus makes You known. Cause us to ever remain on the trail of faith through this present wilderness, upon which Jesus has blazed the way. Also, please use Your Spirit to encourage us through the Supper to remember both Christ's sacrifice and that He alone is the way, the name, and the person through Whom we must come to draw near to You. And it is in Jesus' name that we pray. Amen.

54. The Sanctity of Life

For God so loved the world, that he gave his only Son, that whoever believes in him should not perish but have eternal life.
JOHN 3:16

PRINCIPLE:

From time to time we look into God's Word concerning the sanctity of life and its inestimable value to God. One of the crucial ways we see the unfathomable value of human life in God's sight is through the unfathomable price He was willing to pay to redeem many of our own image-bearing human lives. The ultimate argument for Christians to be strongly prolife is the Good News of God's Gospel in Jesus Christ.

Although original sin and our own sinful proclivities had separated us from God and marred the image-bearing we were created to accomplish, the Lord nevertheless set His heart upon us from before the foundation of the world and determined to rescue our lives from eternal death through the one-time death of His one and only Son, Jesus Christ. Father, Son, and Holy Spirit covenanted together to redeem God's elect image-bearers. This is truly the heart of the Gospel, the promise of eternal salvation for all who have saving faith in Jesus' redeeming blood.

Through the gift of saving faith in Jesus alone, we are delivered from eternal condemnation and spiritual death, even as we receive the promise of everlasting life and the great and certain hope of the resurrection of our physical bodies one day at King Jesus' return. It is in and through Jesus that we are able to perceive how great the Father's love toward us truly is.

And so as we consider what God was determined to do — the price He was determined to pay — to save many lives from everlasting death, we have yet more astounding proof of the sanctity of life to our Lord and our God! It is therefore clearly evident that human lives are precious in God's sight, both in this life and for eternity to come. And as human image-bearers are so very precious — priceless — in the Lord's sight, so also should every human life be in our eyes, from the moment God begins knitting them together in their mother's womb (Psalm 139:12–14) until the divinely-appointed end of their physical lives.

Let's reflect on these profound truths as we celebrate today the newness of life we have in Jesus Christ our risen and life-sustaining Savior and King.

> **PRAYER:**
>
> Our gracious and loving heavenly Father, we thank and praise You for giving to us the gift of everlasting life through faith in the Lord Jesus. We thank You for cherishing the lives You have made in Your image to the point that You would sacrifice Your one and only Son in order to deliver us from our sinful, hopeless condition. As we gather around the table for the Lord's Supper, may we remember how very much You have loved us and continue to love us through Jesus Christ our Lord. And may our worship and our Communion celebration give to You all the praise and the glory. In Jesus' name we pray. Amen.

55. I Am the Bread of Life

When they found him on the other side of the sea, they said to him, "Rabbi, when did you come here?" Jesus answered them, "Truly, truly, I say to you, you are seeking me, not because you saw signs, but because you ate your fill of the loaves. Do not work for the food that perishes, but for the food that endures to eternal life, which the Son of Man will give to you. For on him God the Father has set his seal." Then they said to him, "What must we do, to be doing the works of God?" Jesus answered them, "This is the work of God, that you believe in him whom he has sent." So they said to him, "Then what sign do you do, that we may see and believe you? What work do you perform? Our fathers ate the manna in the wilderness; as it is written, 'He gave them bread from heaven to eat.'" Jesus then said to them, "Truly, truly, I say to you, it was not Moses who gave you the bread from heaven, but my Father gives you the true bread from heaven. For the bread of God is he who comes down from heaven and gives life to the world." They said to him, "Sir, give us this bread always."

Jesus said to them, "I am the bread of life; whoever comes to me shall not hunger, and whoever believes in me shall never thirst."

JOHN 6:25–35

PRINCIPLE:

In the difficult years of traveling in the wilderness between Egypt and the Promised Land, God's people experienced both great hunger and severe thirst. In Exodus 16:12 we read that the Lord heard the grumblings of His people and that He rained down manna from heaven in the morning and quail at twilight. He also directed Moses to the rock at Horeb in Rephidim and caused water to flow. God provided abundantly and miraculously for the physical needs of His people. And in the case of the manna, He provided food perpetually — six days out of every seven throughout their forty-year journey.

Jesus declares in John 6 that those who ate God's miraculous manna in the wilderness later died. However, He also declares that He is the true bread that *comes down from heaven and gives life to the world.* Several times He repeats the revelation that He is the bread of life and that whoever eats of His bread will not die, but will live forever. Those who spiritually feed upon Jesus and drink deeply from the flowing fountain of His life by faith will never hunger or thirst at all.

We have the opportunity with every Lord's Supper celebration to symbolically and spiritually feed upon Christ's body and drink from His cleansing blood. While we do not actually eat and drink the physical body and blood of Christ, as though the bread and the cup have been transformed into the things they symbolize, we do confess that spiritually Jesus is truly present and we do in fact by God's grace eat and drink from the fullness of resurrection life which Jesus has purchased with His sin-bearing body and sin-cleansing blood. The Lord's Supper is a crucial means of God's grace and provision for us. And as we partake of Communion our spiritual hunger and thirst is indeed satisfied by Jesus Christ, the true manner which God sent from heaven — the true rock from which spiritual waters flow!

PRAYER:
Dear Lord, we give You thanks and praise that while we walk along the journey of faith that You have prepared for us in this life, You give us true manna to eat and living water to drink through Jesus Christ, Your Son, our Lord. We also praise You that spiritually Jesus' flesh is our food and Jesus' blood is our satisfying drink. We marvel that although the elements we use to celebrate Your holy Supper, the bread and the cup, do not change into the actual body and blood of Jesus our Savior, we do by the Holy Spirit and Your amazing grace spiritually feed upon the body of Christ and drink His shed blood. Holy Father, satisfy according to Your faithfulness our spiritual hunger and thirst as we draw near to Christ in Communion. Encourage us that You will never leave us nor forsake us. That all along our wilderness journey of faith from salvation to the Promised Land You are always present by Your Spirit, giving us heavenly manna to eat and living waters to drink. We praise You and thank You, in Jesus' name. Amen.

56. The Light, the Life, and the Supper

Again Jesus spoke to them, saying, "I am the light of the world. Whoever follows me will not walk in darkness, but will have the light of life."

JOHN 8:12

PRINCIPLE:

The Apostle John repeatedly identified Jesus as the true light and as the life. He begins in his majestic opening verses of the Gospel deliberately connecting Jesus the Son with the work of creation described in Genesis chapter 1. In doing so, he declares that in Jesus Christ the Word, *was life, and the life was the light of men. The light shines in the darkness, and the darkness has not overcome it.*

This great truth about the Son's identity is underlined in John 8:12 as the Apostle records Jesus' emphatic description of Himself: *I am the light of the world. Whoever follows me will not walk in darkness, but will have the light of life.* Then again, in chapter 9, as Jesus heals a man born blind, He teaches His disciples that, *As long as I am in the world, I am the light of the world.* When we remember that Jesus likely taught these things about Himself during the Feast of Booths, which included an incredibly dramatic light ceremony, the importance of His self-identification as light and life takes on added significance.

Jesus is saying to us that just as He spoke light into the darkness that was over the face of the primordial deep, just as He breathed into man that first breath of life, so also He came into this created world — a world darkened by sin and death — in order to bring eternal light and life. Jesus the Son reveals to us in His incarnation, life, death, resurrection, and ascension the glory of God the Father and His marvelous redemptive plan to reverse the darkness that brought the curse. Christ's heavenly illumination, conveyed by the Holy Spirit, brings His adopted brothers and sisters everlasting life. And for those of us who believe by faith, the Spirit of Christ illumines the Scriptures, much as a pure, bright light enables us to see in the midst of a dark-shrouded night. Jesus' light shines brightly, undimmed, unwaveringly into the darkness on our behalf, and the darkness has not overcome it — and never will!

Let us gather together at the Lord's Table as those who walk in the newness of the light and the life of Jesus Christ. Let us ask the Spirit to show us in the Supper our God, who has indeed *made His face to shine upon [us]*, and *lifted up His countenance upon [us]* (Numbers 6:25–26) through His one and only Son, *the light of the world*. And let us ask the Lord Jesus to continue strengthening us, equipping us, and revealing to us His Word, so that we will never walk in darkness, but always enjoy the light of life.

> **PRAYER:**
>
> Dear Lord, show us this day the light of Christ's glory. Cause us to see Your Son, the light of life, as we partake in the Lord's Supper. Help us to draw near to You by the Holy Spirit even as You draw near to us. And may our Communion together around the Table image the light of the Gospel of Jesus Christ for others to see. May we indeed carry the light of Jesus' Good News with us out into the world after our Sacrament is complete and we have been sent with Your blessing. In Jesus' name. Amen.

57. Jesus, the Resurrection and the Life and the Supper

> *Jesus said to her, "I am the resurrection and the life. Whoever believes in me, though he die, yet shall he live, and everyone who lives and believes in me shall never die. Do you believe this?"*
>
> JOHN 11:25–26

PRINCIPLE:
Jesus reveals Himself to the grieving Martha as the resurrection and the life. And it is to this same Jesus that we also come by faith, acknowledging Him as truly and uniquely the resurrection and the life. It is the divine self-revelation of Christ our Savior that whoever believes in Him, *though he die, yet shall he live.* And so we understand and we cling by faith to the blessed hope contained in this promise — that Jesus will return in glory and that all those who have died in Him will rise in resurrection splendor. Jesus also declares to Martha that, *everyone who lives and believes in me shall never die.* And we understand that this refers to the newness of life we receive when the Holy Spirit comes and dwells within us, regenerating us, and exchanging our hearts of stone for hearts of flesh. Jesus asks a simple question — *Do you believe this?* And indeed, the faith we have received through the Spirit rises up within us to exclaim joyfully and confidently in answer — "Yes indeed!"

    We understand that the promised resurrection and the newness of life we presently enjoy are completely dependent upon and entirely connected with Jesus' atoning work in our place on the cross of Calvary. In the Lord's Supper, Jesus' one-time sacrificial service on our behalf is represented by the bread and cup, which remind us of His sin-bearing body and sin-cleansing blood. Jesus says that our faith and believing* dependence upon Him — our spiritual intimacy with Him must be such that He describes it as though we were *eating* and *drinking* Him! Christ teaches in John 6:54 that, *Whoever feeds on my flesh and drinks my blood has eternal life, and I will raise him up on the last day.*

    Now in saying this Jesus did not teach that when we partake of the Lord's Supper we actually eat and drink the flesh and blood of Christ. Rather, He declares that we must receive Him so fully through the indwelling Holy Spirit, and that our belief must be so inwardly settled, that eating and drinking is an appropriate metaphor or illustration of taking in and being sustained in this new relationship. Jesus does teach us, however, that the bread and the cup in the supper *represent* His body and blood, the benefits of which we have received by faith. And so as we celebrate the Supper, we are reminded through the bread and the cup of the newness of life and the promised resurrection purchased for us by Jesus' suffering body and poured-out blood so long ago. Let us come to the Lord's Table as those who indeed believe that Jesus is the resurrection and the life. And let us come as those who know that *whoever believes in Christ, though he die, yet shall he live, and everyone who lives and believes in Him shall never die.*

*JESUS SPEAKS OF "BELIEF" THREE TIMES IN THIS PASSAGE.

PRAYER:

Lord Jesus, we come to this Communion table knowing that we have everlasting life only because You have given us saving faith in You. We praise You for the work You accomplished on the cross in saving us from eternal death in the fires of hell. We thank You the newness of life we have in You. Although we know that we do not actually feed upon Your flesh or drink Your shed blood in the Supper, we do praise You that we do receive You really and truly spiritually through celebrating Communion. We give You all thanks and praise. In Your saving name we pray. Amen.

58. Washing Each Other's Feet

> *When he had washed their feet and put on his outer garments and resumed his place, he said to them, "Do you understand what I have done to you? You call me Teacher and Lord, and you are right, for so I am. If I then, your Lord and Teacher, have washed your feet, you also ought to wash one another's feet. For I have given you an example, that you also should do just as I have done to you. Truly, truly, I say to you, a servant is not greater than his master, nor is a messenger greater than the one who sent him.*
>
> JOHN 13:12–16

PRINCIPLE:
During our Lord Jesus' last night with His disciples before His betrayal and death, He celebrated one last Passover meal with them. And as part of their Passover gathering Jesus rose from His place of honor as the host of the meal, stripped off His outer garments, wrapped a towel around His waist, and to everyone's surprise, began washing His disciples' feet. This was a truly amazing act of service and of humility for the Son of the living God! It was utterly unheard of for a famous rabbi or teacher among the Jewish people to perform such a menial act — something normally done by the household servants or by the person of lowest status within the group. And yet Jesus of Nazareth, God's Messiah, humbled Himself as a servant and performed this act of simple service for the men He had been discipling for the past three years.

As Jesus began washing the disciples' feet, the Apostle Peter objected strongly that someone of such an honored status should do such debasing, humble work. And yet Jesus declared, *If I do not wash you, you have no share with me.* Peter and the other disciples still had much to learn from Jesus. And much of it had to do with servant leadership. Many of them had longed for a place of honor at Jesus' right hand or left hand when He would be the King of Israel, sitting upon the throne of David. Yet despite Jesus' constant prophecies and clear statements that His path to glory was by way of suffering and the cross, they did not fully understand that the Messiah was also God's suffering servant — that as Jesus came not to be served but to serve, and give His life as a ransom for many, so also those who follow after Him must do the same.

Jesus used this act of simple service — a physical activity that made a strong visual illustration — in order to vividly symbolize what the life of a disciple of Christ should look like. Instead of seeking the highest places of honor and the most lavish of titles or treasure in serving in Christ's kingdom, we are to have the mind of Christ, Who, as Paul wrote in Philippians 2:3–8, was characterized by humility and concern for the interests of others.

Some denominations include the practice of foot washing as part of their worship celebrations. No doubt they see the value in reenacting Christ's humble yet beautiful illustration of the servant heart of a true disciple. Yet it is not necessary to repeat this symbolic act on a regular basis in the church. Rather, what truly delights the heart of God is our true service as loving servants to one another in the body of Christ. As we use the spiritual and physical gifts we have received from God and from the Holy Spirit to meet the needs of our brothers and sisters in Christ, we fulfill this instruction from Jesus that we should wash one another's feet, even as He washed His disciples' feet.

How beautiful is it when the family of God gather together and come to the Lord's Supper as part of Christ-centered worship as those who have ministered and served one another during the days of the previous week — as those who even in that time of prayerful preparation before the Supper think of their love toward Christ and toward one another as one redeemed, kingdom family.

PRAYER:

Our gracious and loving heavenly Father, draw us near to Your Sacrament that we may be reminded anew of the servant-minded humble service of Jesus Christ, Your Son, our Savior. As the Holy Spirit leads us to consider, through the symbols of the bread and the cup, how Christ served, suffered, and died for us, may we also have hearts filled with a desire to humbly serve others as well. In very tangible and practical ways, may we in fact wash one another's feet through acts of charity and helps, as well as the work of prayer, discipling, and fellowship. May our service to one another image Christ Jesus' many humble acts of service for us. And may You be glorified as Your kingdom servants gather around Christ's suffering service Supper. In Jesus' name we pray. Amen.

59. The Spirit of Truth and the Supper

When the Spirit of truth of comes, he will guide you into all the truth, for he will not speak on his own authority, but whatever he hears he will speak, and he will declare to you the things that are to come. He will glorify me, for he will take what is mine and declare it to you. All that the Father has is mine; therefore I said that he will take what is mine and declare it to you.

JOHN 16:13–15

PRINCIPLE:
Our Lord Jesus told the disciples that when He had ascended into heaven, He and the Father would send the Holy Spirit in great power to enable them to *be my witnesses in Jerusalem, and in all Judea, and Samaria, and to the end of the earth* (Acts 1:8). One key aspect of the Holy Spirit's work is to reveal *all the truth*. In fact, we understand from Jesus' words in John 16 that the Holy Spirit is the *Spirit of truth*. The Spirit acts as the revealer of God's truth and the illuminator or guide into that revealed truth, which is the written Word of God.

We depend upon the Holy Spirit to take the inspired words of institution during the Supper, and to make spiritual use of the simple elements of the bread and the cup, to reveal to us inwardly the work of Jesus Christ. The Spirit enables us to truly remember the atonement of Christ as it works effectively on our behalf before the Father's throne. It is also the great gift of the Spirit of God that He makes it possible for Jesus Christ to be spiritually and specially present during the Gospel Feast.

There is also, in this working of the Spirit of truth during the Lord's Supper, a fulfillment of Christ's promise that *he will take what is mine and declare it to you.* The Apostle Paul tells us that *as often as you eat this bread and drink the cup, you proclaim the Lord's death until he comes* (1 Corinthians 11:26). It is the Spirit of Christ that takes the work, benefits, and blessings of Jesus' death and resurrection and declares them to us. Further, the Spirit proclaims Christ to all who are present when the Lord's Supper is observed. We understand that the Spirit works mightily in the proclamation of God's written Word. We also need to understand that He works mightily in the proclamation, visually and sensibly, of Christ as His redeemed believers gather around the Table of the Lord!

PRAYER:

Gracious and loving Heavenly Father, glorious giver of Jesus Christ Your Son, give to us Your Spirit's working today, so that we may truly have proclaimed to us the truth, the work, the benefits, the blessings, and above all, the presence of Jesus with us as we celebrate Communion together. As Your Spirit takes what is Yours and declares it mightily to us, may You and Jesus our Savior be glorified. May we find in His ministry to us *the things that are to come*, our blessed future hope, the return of Christ in power, and authority, and glory, when all of the redeemed will enjoy perpetual Communion with You. O holy Father, how lavishly You give to us Your children through the ministry of the Spirit of Christ! In Jesus' name we pray. Amen.

60. Oneness in Jesus Displayed in the Supper

> *I do not ask for these only, but also for those who will believe in me through their word, that they may all be one, just as you, Father, are in me, and I in you, that they also may be in us, so that the world may believe that you have sent me. The glory that you have given me I have given to them, that they may be one even as we are one, I in them and you in me, that they may become perfectly one, so that the world may know that you sent me and loved them even as you loved me.*
>
> JOHN 17:20–23

PRINCIPLE:

In the church I currently pastor, for our regular services of worship we use a small token of fellowship in Christ that comes from the Caribbean. It is a cup for the Lord's Supper, made by hand in the island nation of Haiti, where our brothers and sisters in Christ also gather to pray and praise, hear the Word of God proclaimed, and celebrate the Sacrament of the Lord's Supper.

This small token from Haiti serves to visually remind our congregation of our oneness in the Holy Spirit, our shared faith in Christ Jesus, and our union together in the body with our Haitian covenant family. Among the churches ministered to by Jesus through our missionary partners, there are added daily many Haitians to the body of Christ, the Church. And as these believers gather together to worship the risen Lord, they lift up powerful prayers of intercession for us. What a beautiful, fragrant picture of unity in the Spirit, much as Jesus asked the Father for in John 17.

Every celebration of the Lord's Supper visually declares to us the Gospel of Jesus Christ and the oneness we enjoy in Him through the presence of His Holy Spirit. Our testimony to the reality of the saving work of Jesus Christ is in part made manifest through our unity in Him. Jesus prayed that we may become perfectly one, so that the world may know that God sent Jesus His Son and loved us even as the Father loved the Son. While we receive Communion, let's remember our shared oneness in Christ with each other in our fellowship in Christ's local body, and also remember our oneness in Jesus through the Spirit with our Haitian brothers and sisters, and with believers the world over.

PRAYER:

Heavenly Father, help us to see in the Supper our oneness with You and our oneness with one another as Your covenant family in Jesus Christ our Savior. Lead us by Your Spirit to put aside all malice and bitterness toward one another that there may be no divisions among us as we share together in the bread and the cup. May our oneness around the Communion table fulfill Jesus' High Priestly Prayer that we would be one even as You and the Son are one. We make this prayer in the blessed name of Jesus. Amen.

61. The Father's Cup and the Lord's Supper

So Jesus said to Peter, "Put your sword into its sheath; shall I not drink the cup that the Father has given me?"

JOHN 18:11

PRINCIPLE:

There is an intimate and unbreakable connection between the cup, which the Father gave the Son to drink, and the cup, which we bless and receive during the Lord's Supper. For Jesus our Savior, the Father's cup was most bitter and terrible, for its contents were utterly saturated with our vile and wicked sins, mixed to the uttermost with the holy and fierce wrath of God. It is no wonder then that the holy and sinless Son of God recoiled and was *very sorrowful, even to death.*

We can sense Jesus' deep suffering, along with His unswerving and faithful commitment to His Father in the pleading prayer He uttered three times that terrible night in Gethsemane: *My Father, if it be possible, let this cup pass from me; nevertheless, not as I will, but as you will* (Matthew 26:39*ff*). And Jesus did indeed obediently drink the Father's bitter cup to the very last drop as His blood was poured out to satisfy the righteous judgment of God the Father toward our sins. Jesus consumed every moment of the eternity in Hell which had been reserved for our just punishment from God.

On the very same night that Jesus received the Father's cup of judgment, the Son offered to His disciples and all who would come after them in faith an entirely different cup. At the end of the Passover meal, our Lord raised the cup of blessing and declared, *This cup that is poured out for you is the new covenant in my blood* (Luke 22:20). While Jesus Christ drank to the very bottom the awful cup of the Father's wrath and our sin, He filled to overflowing the cup of God's marvelous grace for us to drink. The cup we drink is, according to Jesus Himself, the new covenant in His precious blood. This is the Covenant of Redemption applied by God to You and to me and all who believe through Jesus the Son. And now we both celebrate and remember, as the Apostle Paul exhorts the believers in Corinth, to *Do this, as often as you drink it, in remembrance of me.*

With each celebration of the Lord's Supper, the cup that we bless serves to remind us of the Father's bitter, bitter cup of condemnation which the Son humbly drank in our place. Jesus received our sins and the Father's just wrath, while we by faith receive the forgiveness and gracious covenant blessings of God in Christ! The bread and the cup we receive in the Supper are vivid pictures of what Jesus endured for our eternal sakes. Let us indeed receive this means of God's grace by the powerful working in us of His most Holy Spirit through the Gospel Feast!

> **PRAYER:**
>
> Dear Lord Jesus, thank You for drinking the terrible cup of the Father's great and just wrath for our sin, so that we would not have to drink it ourselves. We praise you that in place of the cup of God's wrath You have given to us the cup of the new covenant in Your blood — the cup, in fact, of God the Father's great and eternal blessings for all who believe in Your name. May we now see the reality of this wonderful exchange of cups as we celebrate the Gospel Feast during our Sabbath day worship. And in all these things we give You the honor, the praise, and the glory. Amen.

62. He Will Return

> *He said to them, "It is not for you to know times or seasons that the Father has fixed by his own authority. But you will receive power when the Holy Spirit has come upon you, and you will be my witnesses in Jerusalem and in all Judea and Samaria, and to the end of the earth." And when he had said these things, as they were looking on, he was lifted up, and a cloud took him out of their sight. And while they were gazing into heaven as he went, behold, two men stood by them in white robes, and said, "Men of Galilee, why do you stand looking into heaven? This Jesus, who was taken up from you into heaven, will come in the same way as you saw him go into heaven."*
>
> ACTS 1:7–11

PRINCIPLE:

There are two things powerfully declared to those who watched Jesus ascend into heaven and declared by revelation of God's Word to all those who believe in Christ. The first of these two truths is that with the ascension of Christ, the Holy Spirit was given a broader mission and poured out on all who come to faith in Jesus, transforming them and empowering them for kingdom work.

The second of these truths so precious to believers is that just as Jesus ascended into heaven and was received by the heavenly court with great honor and glory — seated beside His Father in power and authority — so also will our Savior one day return in the same way at the consummation of the new heaven and new earth. At that glorious second appearing of Christ, we will join Him in triumphal procession as He assumes the fullness of His reign upon the earth and we enjoy His presence forevermore in resurrected glory.

It is also these two truths that expand our appreciation of the Lord's Supper. The Spirit of Christ is the One who empowers our remembrance of Jesus' atoning death and His glorious resurrection. The Holy Spirit's presence with us ever reminds us of Jesus' ascension into heaven, while the Father makes all His enemies a footstool for His feet. And as we often observe when we gather around the Table, Christ is coming again one day and on that day, we who believe will be like Him, for we will be able to see Him fully, as those redeemed and resurrected to everlasting life.

The Sacrament of Communion is a time in which the Holy Spirit reminds us of Christ's completed work, His ongoing presence and empowerment with us today, and the encouragement and hope of Jesus' glorious return. The Spirit, poured out on Pentecost after Jesus' ascension, sustains us in Christ, and at the Lord's Supper feeds us upon the marvelous grace of God.

PRAYER:
Heavenly Father, although we were not standing on the mount with the Apostles watching Jesus ascend into heaven, we do thank You and praise You that at Jesus' glorious return we will see Him coming in the clouds and with great power and majesty. Every time we celebrate the Lord's Supper, Your servant the Apostle Paul reminds us that *we proclaim the Lord's death until He comes*. Please build up within us a joyful anticipation of the fulfillment of the blessed hope — which is the return of Jesus Christ in triumph. And it is in Jesus' name that we ask this. Amen.

63. Repent and Believe

> *Now when they heard this they were cut to the heart, and said to Peter and the rest of the apostles, "Brothers, what shall we do?" And Peter said to them, "Repent and be baptized every one of you in the name of Jesus Christ for the forgiveness of your sins, and you will receive the gift of the Holy Spirit. For the promise is for you and for your children and for all who are far off, everyone whom the Lord our God calls to himself." And with many other words he bore witness and continued to exhort them, saying, "Save yourselves from this crooked generation." So those who received his word were baptized, and there were added that day about three thousand souls.*
>
> ACTS 2:37–41

PRINCIPLE:

Peter's great, Spirit-anointed sermon to the crowds gathered in Jerusalem on the day of Pentecost represents the very heart of the Gospel offer of salvation through faith in Jesus Christ. God mightily used the powerful truths of His Good News in bringing 3,000 people from all over the known world to faith in Jesus His Son on that very day. And the harvest of souls at Pentecost was just the beginning of the mighty, kingdom-building process the Lord continues even today through His preachers, teachers, missionaries, evangelists, and every believer who shares his or her faith.

The Apostle Peter, empowered by the Holy Spirit, declared on that day so long ago the absolute necessity of repentance, of receiving the covenant sign of baptism, of looking in faith to Jesus Christ for forgiveness of sins, and of receiving the indwelling power of the Spirit of Christ. These are the essentials of the faith we profess today as well. They are the basis for every evangelistic opportunity and every mission project.

But Peter also told the gathered crowd that the promises of God to redeem His chosen people through Jesus Christ were not only for them. The promises were also for their children *and for all who are far off, everyone whom the Lord our God calls to himself.* And so from the Apostle we learn that the Good News of Jesus Christ is declared in a multi-generational context. Its promises are also unbounded by the passage of time. Until the Lord Jesus Christ returns in glory, each and every generation will hear the Gospel and many in each generation will come to saving faith as the Lord exercises His calling upon them.

As we come to the Lord's Supper, let us bear in mind and heart the central message of the Gospel of Jesus Christ, which calls us to repentance, to membership in the visible body of Christ, to faithful dependence upon Jesus, and to appropriating, by faith, the sanctification and ongoing enabling of God's Holy Spirit, which now dwells within us. Let us also consider that the feast we celebrate in honor of Christ, connects us to those who have walked by faith before us in years long gone by, and also connects us to those generations who are yet to come — generations who will by faith call upon the same Lord Jesus and celebrate their communion with Him and with us, by means of this Lord's Supper.

PRAYER:

Lord Jesus, we give thanks for the way You used Your servant Peter to proclaim the pure Gospel, repent and be baptized in the name of Jesus for the forgiveness of sins and you will be saved. We also give You praise that the Good News about You was not limited to Peter's generation or any other generation for that matter, but is a certain promise to us, and to our children, and to those who are far off, everyone whom the Lord our God calls to Himself. We ask now that the Holy Spirit will give us greater understanding of these truths as we receive the Lord's Supper. May we know by faith that Your kingdom and Your Gospel embrace people of faith from every generation. May our celebrations of Communion display the past, present, and future glories of Your kingdom. Amen.

64. The Lord's Day and the Lord's Supper

On the first day of the week, when we were gathered together to break bread, Paul talked with them, intending to depart on the next day, and he prolonged his speech until midnight.

ACTS 20:7

PRINCIPLE:

When the Apostle Paul arrived in Troas, on the coast of what is now called Turkey, he met with the gathered believers and his traveling companions on the first day of the week — Sunday — for the breaking of bread and for the preaching of the Gospel. The expression *to break bread* is used throughout the New Testament to indicate the early congregations' fellowship or agape meals, which included the Sacrament of the Lord's Supper. These celebrations on the first day of the week were connected with preaching and teaching of the Word of God, as well as with other activities of worship. This is the worship-fellowship celebration we also have described in Acts 2:42:

And they devoted themselves to the apostles' teaching and fellowship, to the breaking of bread and the prayers.

While most churches today no longer share in a full fellowship meal featuring the Lord's Supper as a conclusion to Lord's Day worship, the divinely ordained pattern is preserved wherever and whenever the proclamation of the Word is audibly and visually declared through preaching and through the Sacrament of Communion. When we are joined together on the Christian Sabbath for morning worship, our celebration of God's gift of salvation through Jesus is heightened when we conclude our service of worship celebration as He has instructed — united around His table as one redeemed covenant family — doing this in remembrance of Him. Today many Christians might object to a weekly observance because partaking of the Supper frequently means that our services of worship might run longer than usual. And yet this seemed to be no problem for the church of believers in Troas! May the Holy Spirit do His work in us, creating such a longing in our hearts for the special presence of Christ in worship and for the means of grace God has provided in the Lord's Supper such that we might be less enslaved to time and more enraptured by Christ.

PRAYER:

O gracious and loving heavenly Father, by Your Holy Spirit, please bless our gathering together for the Lord's Supper. May our breaking of bread and drinking from the cup truly, by faith, display the wonderful work of Jesus Christ, Your Son and our Savior. Help us to find such joy and wonder in Christ through this Sacrament that we are never tempted to neglect participating, or simply coming to Your table as an empty religious ritual. May we always find our Communion celebration to be a place of spiritual nourishment by Your grace. Through Your Word and by the Spirit of Christ draw us with eagerness to this Gospel Feast. And may Your Spirit work such love for You within us, that we pay no attention to the length of our worship this beautiful Sabbath day, that it in fact may seem for us to be a blessed foretaste of eternal glorified worship of You, the Son, and the Spirit. In Jesus' name. Amen.

65. Called to Belong to Jesus

> *Paul, a servant of Christ Jesus, called to be an apostle, set apart for the gospel of God, which he promised beforehand through his prophets in the holy Scriptures, concerning his Son, who was descended from David according to the flesh and was declared to be the Son of God in power according to the Spirit of holiness by his resurrection from the dead, Jesus Christ our Lord, through whom we have received grace and apostleship to bring about the obedience of faith for the sake of his name among all the nations, including you who are called to belong to Jesus Christ,...*
>
> ROMANS 1:1–6

PRINCIPLE:
The Apostle Paul begins his inspired letter to the congregation of believers in Rome with a marvelous greeting. It was the normal practice when writing correspondence in that time to begin, not with the addressee's name and information, but rather with an introduction concerning the writer of the letter. What sets Paul's greetings in many of his letters apart is their inspired revelation of the glorious Gospel of Christ.

Paul writes of the prophetic work of the spokesmen for God throughout the Old Testament revelation, who pointed the people's faith to the coming Messiah. Then his greeting revels in the incarnation of the Son through the line of King David, and His victorious resurrection from the dead *according to the Spirit of holiness*. Finally, it unfolds the implications of Jesus' completed work, as it is applied to the chosen people of God.

As we come to the Lord's Supper it is particularly worth noting that Paul writes in his greeting that as a result of Christ's work, *we have received grace... to bring about the obedience of faith for the sake of his name among all the nations, including you who are called to belong to Jesus Christ*. We see the Lord's Supper as one of God's marvelous means of grace — a means which when taken according to saving faith — provides fortifying grace to nourish our minds, hearts, and souls concerning the Lord Jesus Christ.

As those who are called to belong to Jesus Christ, we are called to gather around His table and to both remember and celebrate His coming, His atoning sacrifice, His resurrection, and His ongoing redemptive work for us and all the elect children of God.

> **PRAYER:**
>
> Heavenly Father, we thank and praise You because in Jesus and by faith You have called us out of darkness and into Your marvelous light. You have called us to belong to You through Christ Jesus Your Son. We also now thank and praise You that in addition to the abundant grace You have shown us in Jesus, You continue to shower Your equipping and sustaining graces upon us every day, and especially so when we pray, hear Your Word preached, or receive the Sacrament of Communion. Father, please bless us and feed us as we partake of the bread and of the cup. Strengthen our faith and our reliance upon Jesus. Make us more fully vessels of Your grace that others may see Jesus in us and bearing good fruit within our lives. In Jesus' name we pray. Amen.

66. From Faith for Faith

> *For I am not ashamed of the gospel, for it is the power of God for salvation to everyone who believes, to the Jew first and also to the Greek. For in it the righteousness of God is revealed from faith for faith, as it is written, "The righteous shall live by faith."*
> ROMANS 1:16–17

PRINCIPLE:
Just as the Apostle Paul writes to the Roman believers, the basis for our justification is the completed work of Jesus Christ on our behalf, applied to us by God through the means of the gift of faith, birthed in our hearts through the work of the Holy Spirit. The central significance of justification is that, through no merit or worthiness on our own part, the righteousness of God in Christ is credited — or judicially declared — to belong to us. Our justification, entirely according to the merciful choosing of God, is inseparable from our salvation. In order to receive the justification — the legal declaration of God that we are righteous [in Christ] — we must first receive the gift of saving faith in Him. Faith is THE essential requirement necessary for spiritually dead sinners to receive everlasting life in Christ.

Similarly, it is absolutely necessary that in order to receive the fortifying grace provided at the Lord's Supper, we must approach the King's Table with true, Spirit-birthed faith in Jesus Christ. The *Westminster Confession of Faith* puts it this way:

Worthy receivers, outwardly partaking of the visible elements, in this sacrament, do then also, inwardly by faith, really and indeed, yet not carnally and corporately but spiritually, receive and feed upon, Christ crucified, and all the benefits of his death, the body and blood of Christ being then, not corporally or carnally, in, with, or under the bread and wine; yet, as really, but spiritually, present to the faith of believers in that ordinance, as the elements themselves are to their outward senses.

Without genuine faith in the Lord Jesus Christ, partaking of the Lord's Supper is merely an outward liturgical ritual, offering no spiritual benefit and in fact incurring greater wrath and judgment from God. The Apostle Paul writes of the Gospel, describing it as *the power of God for salvation to everyone who believes*. And indeed, that is precisely what the Good News represents. Note the similarities between what

Paul said of the Gospel in Romans 1 and what the *Westminster Shorter Catechism*, question 91, says of the Sacrament of the Lord's Supper:

Question: How do the sacraments become effectual means of salvation?

Answer: The sacraments become effectual means of salvation, not from any virtue in them, or in him that doth administer them; but only by the blessing of Christ, and the working of His Spirit in them that by faith receive them.

Thus, the crucial element in order for believers to receive God's grace through receiving the Lord's Supper, is not the piety or practice of the pastor, not the physical elements themselves, but rather the presence of genuine, Spirit-birthed faith unto salvation in those who receive it.

PRAYER:

Our Lord and our God, please guide us into true worship and adoration of You. By Your Holy Spirit and through genuine saving faith bring us into sweet Communion celebration with You and with our brothers and sisters in Christ. As Your Spirit works through our Supper celebration, may we truly feed upon Jesus Christ by faith — spiritually, not physically, and yet truly and powerfully. Holy and loving Father, we thank You and praise You for this means of feeding us according to Your grace, strengthening our faith and our desire to share that faith in confidence and joy with others In Jesus' name we pray. Amen.

67. A Child of God Inwardly

> *For no one is a Jew who is merely one outwardly, nor is circumcision outward and physical. But a Jew is one inwardly, and circumcision is a matter of the heart, by the Spirit, not by the letter. His praise is not from man but from God.*
>
> ROMANS 2:28–29

PRINCIPLE:
The Apostle Paul concludes chapter 2 of his letter to the believers in Rome, by reminding them that having all of the outward signs of membership in the people of God does not automatically make someone a truly redeemed covenant child. It is only through the working of God the Father in giving His Holy Spirit into the heart of someone that they genuinely become an inward bearer of true covenant membership.

Paul declares that the visible, physical sign of circumcision does not profit a person at all unless they have been inwardly circumcised through the sovereign working of God's Spirit, originating from faith in the atoning sacrifice of Jesus Christ. To be counted among the Israel of God; men, women, and children must be transformed in their hearts according to the grace and mercy of God in Christ.

In a similar way, the receiving of the Lord's Supper will profit us nothing if we simply receive it as an outward, visible ritual. We must by faith understand that the Spirit of God is at work during our celebration of the Lord's Supper — inwardly — and that He uses this simply outward sign to supply us with fortifying grace, drawing our hearts and minds more closely to the sacrifice Jesus our Lord made once for all time on our behalf at Calvary.

Mere outward profession of faith, formal membership in the visible Church, or ritualistic receiving of the Sacrament, without true inward regeneration by the graciousness of God in Christ, will result not only in lack of blessing, but also in greater judgment. It is therefore so important that we come to this table of the Lord by means of true, saving faith alone. When we do come as those redeemed in Jesus, all the marvelous benefits and blessings of the Covenant of Redemption are richly brought to our remembrance and we are encouraged and strengthened for living out our faith in a not fully restored creation. May the celebration of the Lord's Supper be of great blessing to you!

PRAYER:

Heavenly Father, we thank You for making us Your children inwardly, not simply in outward ritualistic practices but in terms of born again, transformed hearts and minds. We praise You for giving us the free gift of saving faith in Jesus Your Son. May the Holy Spirit work in us so that we celebrate Communion as genuine fellowship with You and with everyone adopted into Your covenant family. May the Lord's Supper never be an empty ritual for us, but rather one of the rich means of Your powerful grace. In Jesus' name we pray. Amen.

68. Justified in His Sight

For by works of the law no human being will be justified in his sight, since through the law comes knowledge of sin.

ROMANS 3:20

PRINCIPLE:

The Apostle Paul clearly teaches us that in no way whatsoever can we be saved by our own works and by keeping of the Law of God. Instead, Paul declares to us that the primary purpose of the Law is to display the glorious, holy character of God and expose by contrast our own sinfulness. As we are measured according to the Law's pure standards, we are indeed without excuse before a perfectly righteous God!

It is precisely this realization — that no fallen human being can be justified in the sight of God through the Law — which drives us to seek the Lord Jesus Christ. He is the one and only justifier for those who been given faith in Him. Rather than depending upon our own inability to keep the Law of God, we depend by faith alone on Jesus' perfect obedience to the Law and His righteousness. In doing so, we are declared justified — righteous — according to the righteousness of God in Christ!

And this divine act of justification is exactly what the Apostle writes in the next two verses in Romans 3, verses 21–22:

But now the righteousness of God has been manifested apart from the law, although the Law and the Prophets bear witness to it — the righteousness of God through faith in Jesus Christ for all who believe.

The Lord's Supper visually declares this great Gospel news to us each time we partake by faith. We are reminded that our salvation and our justification was not earned by our own merit or our own works and keeping of God's Law. Instead, our salvation and our justification were purchased for us by the shedding of the life-blood of our Lord and Savior Jesus Christ. It is His perfect obedience and atoning death which allow us to stand excused before God and clothed in His spotless robes!

We can never be reminded too often that we have been redeemed entirely and utterly according to the electing grace of God through the one-time sacrifice of Jesus His Son. Both the preached Word and the Word made visible through the Sacrament of the Supper are powerful instruments in the hands of our Father to underline for us the cost of our eternal redemption — a cost in which we played no part!

> **PRAYER:**
>
> Holy Lord, we bow before You in awe and wonder over Your marvelous and mysterious plan to save us from our sin. We thank You that since we could in no way justify ourselves in Your sight, You chose to declare us righteous by applying the perfect, sinlessness of Jesus Your Son to us by faith. We praise You for the Lord's Supper and its regular reminder to us, through the words of institution and through the bread and the cup, just what it cost You and the Lord Jesus to accomplish our justification and eternal salvation. May the reality of Your great redemption of sinners like us constantly be brought to mind. And may we always rejoice in You the God of our salvation. In Jesus' name. Amen.

69. Blessed Is the One Whose Sins Are Covered

> *What then shall we say was gained by Abraham, our forefather according to the flesh? For if Abraham was justified by works, he has something to boast about, but not before God. For what does the Scripture say? "Abraham believed God, and it was counted to him as righteousness." Now to the one who works, his wages are not counted as a gift but as his due. And to the one who does not work but believes in him who justifies the ungodly, his faith is counted as righteousness, just as David also speaks of the blessing of the one to whom God counts righteousness apart from works:*
>
> *"Blessed are those whose lawless deeds are forgiven, and whose sins are covered; blessed is the man against whom the Lord will not count his sin."*
>
> ROMANS 4:1–8

PRINCIPLE:

Throughout the early chapters of Romans, the Apostle Paul is burdened to declare to his Jewish brethren that the righteousness of God does not come to sinful men through keeping the Law of God. It is the *law of faith*, Paul writes, which is apart from the Old Testament Law and Prophets, that is the means by which God credits His righteousness to sinful men.

Faith is not something that we merit or that we can work to earn, any more than we can work or merit to receive God's righteousness. The only way for sinful, fallen human beings to have their unrighteousness removed and replaced with the righteousness of God is through the gift of faith — faith placed entirely and exclusively in Jesus Christ.

Through God's gift to us of saving faith in Jesus Christ, our *lawless deeds are forgiven, and our sins are covered; blessed are those of us in Jesus against whom the Lord will not count our sin!* In what we call *the great transfer*, our unrighteousness is transferred to Jesus, while His righteousness is transferred to us, through what we call the process of God's justification.

This transfer is brought to our remembrance when we come to the Lord's Table. The unleavened bread reminds us of the sinless body of Christ who bore our sins away upon Himself, And the cup reminds us of His drinking of the cup of God's wrath to the very bitterest of the dregs lying on the bottom, taking upon Himself the chastisement due to each of us for our sins. In the cup we also comprehend the cleansing and covenant-sealing shed blood of Christ. What wonders of our redemption are displayed when we gather around the Table and *proclaim the Lord's death until He comes!*

> **PRAYER:**
> Dear Lord Jesus, indeed we praise You for the greatest of blessings that You have given to us, that those of us who believe in You no longer bear the penalty for our sins. We give thanks that You faithfully came and fulfilled the Father's will by dying on that cross on Calvary and washing away our sins by Your shed blood. We are so thankful, Lord Jesus, that You have set us free from bondage to sin and to sin's curse. As we come to the Supper help us by Your Spirit to see the power of this *great transfer*, by which You have taken our sins upon Yourself and borne them away on that cross, while also giving to us Your righteousness by the declaration and will of God Almighty. We love You because You first loved us and gave Your life as our eternal ransom. With our hearts full of thanksgiving we pray in Your beautiful name. Amen.

70. Counted to Him as Righteousness

> *That is why his [Abraham's] faith was "counted to him as righteousness." But the words "it was counted to him" were not written for his sake alone, but for ours also. It will be counted to us who believe in him who raised from the dead Jesus our Lord, who was delivered up for our trespasses and raised for our justification.*
>
> ROMANS 4:22–25

PRINCIPLE:

The Apostle Paul continues in this part of chapter 4 teaching the believers in Rome that the means by which they are justified in God's holy sight is by means of faith in Jesus Christ alone. In order to underline his point more forcefully, the Apostle continues to hold forth Father Abraham as the paramount example of justification through faith alone.

This is so important for us as believers in Jesus Christ because we are justified in the very same way as our spiritual father Abraham. The righteousness of God Most High is counted to us, as to Abraham, as we, *believe in him who raised from the dead Jesus our Lord*. The object of our faith is our Triune God. We put our trust in the Lord Jesus Christ the Son of God, who came and died for all the elect. We profess God our Father, who raised the Lord Jesus from the dead. And we depend upon God the Holy Spirit as the source of our faith and the One who unites us always to Christ.

At the conclusion of Paul's argument in chapter 4, the Apostle reminds us that the work of the Lord Jesus Christ accomplished two things, along with many others he speaks of elsewhere. First he declares that the Lord Jesus was delivered over to death in order to pay the penalty for our sins. In His death, Christ Jesus bore our sins and stains in His sinless body. In doing so, both the stain and the wrath of God were removed from everyone who believes in Jesus by faith alone.

The second accomplishment of Christ that Paul reminds his readers about is the importance of the resurrection. He says that in Jesus' glorious resurrection, believers in Him were justified. You see, in order to stand in covenant relationship with our holy God, we must not only be *clean* — free of sin and its consequences. We must also be righteous — holy — set apart — perfect in the sight of God. Of course, we can never of ourselves in this life, achieve such an amazing standard. Yet through the resurrection of Jesus, the righteousness of Christ is *counted* or credited to us as we rest in Him according to faith.

The Lord's Supper is a weekly reminder for us of these things. We gaze upon the bread and through the eyes of faith we are reminded that when the Lord Jesus Christ was nailed to that cross, bled, and died, He was bearing in His sinless body our great sin and shame. The cup reminds us of His cleansing blood, by which our stains were removed forever. We bear neither the stain nor the curse of spiritual death any longer.

We also remember that, although the morning after He instituted the Supper, He bled and died for our sins, He also was raised by God the Father from the dead on the third day. And that resurrection is God's sign and seal that Christ's atonement was accepted on our behalf, and that we are now robed in the righteousness of the Lord Jesus Christ. As we come to Communion, let us rejoice in all that Jesus has accomplished for our eternal salvation, by means of His atoning sacrifice, and by means of the gift of faith!

PRAYER:
Our gracious and loving heavenly Father, we delight in the marvelous and powerful resurrection of Jesus Christ as we prepare to partake of Your Gospel Feast. We know by faith that in Jesus' resurrection His substitutionary atonement for us was accepted by You once and for all. And as we consider our Lord Jesus' resurrection we wonder at the joyful news that Christ's perfect righteousness has now been credited to us through the means of Your gift of saving faith in Him. Father, we thank and praise and honor, and declare Your glory as the God Who has saved us and Who has called us into eternal communion with You. We worship You, Father, Son, and Holy Spirit. Amen.

71. Saved by the Offered Life of the Son

> *Therefore, since we have been justified by faith, we have peace with God through our Lord Jesus Christ. Through him we have also obtained access by faith into this grace in which we stand, and we rejoice in hope of the glory of God. More than that, we rejoice in our sufferings, knowing that suffering produces endurance, and endurance produces character, and character produces hope, and hope does not put us to shame, because God's love has been poured into our hearts through the Holy Spirit who has been given to us. For while we were still weak, at the right time Christ died for the ungodly. For one will scarcely die for a righteous person—though perhaps for a good person one would dare even to die—but God shows his love for us in that while we were still sinners, Christ died for us. Since, therefore, we have now been justified by his blood, much more shall we be saved by him from the wrath of God. For if while we were enemies we were reconciled to God by the death of his Son, much more, now that we are reconciled, shall we be saved by his life. More than that, we also rejoice in God through our Lord Jesus Christ, through whom we have now received reconciliation.*
>
> ROMANS 5:1–11

PRINCIPLE:

Here Paul gives to us a marvelous, inspired presentation of the Good News, which is ours by faith in Jesus Christ! Every aspect of the Lord's work in our salvation is displayed for us in these verses. Paul begins with our justification by faith, leading to peace with God through Christ. He then reveals that this justification by faith gives us access to God and hope in His glory. Sanctification by God's grace is described, as is the gift of the Holy Spirit and the love of God.

While we are gathered for the Lord's Supper, let us reflect upon the great grace of God poured out upon us by means of the Holy Spirit and the application of Christ's completed work. Let us also prayerfully ask the Lord for the opening of our hearts and our minds to recognize during the celebration of Communion the reconciliation we have received through our Lord Jesus Christ. And not only are we reconciled to God. We are also saved by His Son's life. All of this was accomplished for God's elect, as Paul says, when *Christ died for us.*

May the written Word of God declared, and the visual-tactile Word of God through the Supper, work together among us as the redeemed people of God to encourage us in the Gospel of Jesus Christ, according to His amazing grace and the powerful working of the Holy Spirit! Also, may both these means of grace be used mightily by the Lord to bring His chosen ones to salvation, according to His providential timing.

> **PRAYER:**
> Our gracious and loving heavenly Father, thank you for removing the great wall of separation which divided us from Your loving presence. Thank You for reconciling us to You through Jesus Christ, Your Son. We pray that You will remind us powerfully through the words of institution and through the elements we share of the life, death, and resurrection of Jesus Christ and its immediate and eternal effects in transforming our lives by Your Spirit. Bless this meal and this fellowship around the Table, we pray, in Jesus' mighty name. Amen.

72. Jesus Christ Abounded for Us

> *But the free gift is not like the trespass. For if many died through one man's trespass, much more have the grace of God and the free gift by the grace of that one man Jesus Christ abounded for many. And the free gift is not like the result of that one man's sin. For the judgment following one trespass brought condemnation, but the free gift following many trespasses brought justification. For if, because of one man's trespass, death reigned through that one man, much more will those who receive the abundance of grace and the free gift of righteousness reign in life through the one man Jesus Christ.*
>
> ROMANS 5:15–17

PRINCIPLE:
As we sit under this portion of the Word of God, let's ask the Spirit of the living God to work its amazing message deeply into our hearts and our minds. In our churches' regular Sabbath morning congregational worship, we exalt the *Second Adam*, the Lord Jesus Christ, in both the Word preached and also the Word made visible through the Lord's Supper.

The Apostle Paul tells us that although the original sin of Adam brought the curse of death and eternal condemnation, the perfect obedience, righteousness, and atoning death of the Lord Jesus Christ brought the gift of justification and eternal life by means of faith by grace for many.

Our celebration of Communion underlines for us this central work of redemption accomplished by Christ Jesus. The context of the Supper originally was the night on which the Lord Jesus was betrayed into the hands of sinners, and it led the next day to Calvary and His atoning work, assuming the sins of God's elect as He died upon the cross.

Our Lord instituted the sacramental meal within the setting of the Passover celebration, for He Himself became our Passover Lamb. In His perfect, one-time sacrifice, the Son of God purchased our redemption from God's wrath and curse, clothing us in this great *transfer* in His own perfect righteousness. For those who believe in Jesus alone for salvation, the original sin curse passed down through Adam, as well as our own individual sinful guilt, is taken away. This is the great beauty displayed visually in the Lord Supper and brought to our hearts and minds by His Spirit and according to His grace. Thanks be to God Most High for the gift of the Second Adam, our Lord and Savior Jesus Christ!

> **PRAYER:**
>
> Dear Lord Jesus, we praise You and honor You because while we were yet sinners, You died for us in order to save us from sin and eternal judgment. In doing so You made the way for us into everlasting life. We thank You for being our Second Adam, the one Who perfectly fulfilled the Father's Law and went to the cross without sin, yet taking upon Yourself our many sins. We ask You by Your Spirit to empower us to come to the Supper by living faith and to receive Your gracious blessings as we eat the bread and drink from the cup. May we come to understand and embrace Your love and sacrifice for us more fully as we meditate upon Your body and blood displayed in the elements of Communion. In Jesus' name we pray. Amen.

73. Brought From Death to Life

> *We know that Christ, being raised from the dead, will never die again; death no longer has dominion over him. For the death he died he died to sin, once for all, but the life he lives he lives to God. So you also must consider yourselves dead to sin and alive to God in Christ Jesus. Let not sin therefore reign in your mortal body, to make you obey its passions. Do not present your members to sin as instruments for unrighteousness, but present yourselves to God as those who have been brought from death to life, and your members to God as instruments for righteousness. For sin will have no dominion over you, since you are not under law but under grace.*
>
> ROMANS 6:9–14

PRINCIPLE:

The Apostle Paul argues in this part of his letter to the believers in Rome that they are to image the Lord Jesus Christ in the manner in which they live their lives. Likewise, all of us who call upon Jesus by faith are to image Him in holiness of living as well. Now of course we cannot do this in our own strength or abilities, anymore than the brothers and sisters in the congregation of first century Rome. In order to live as befits the redeemed of Christ, we must again and again, day after day, appropriate the power of Christ imparted by the Holy Spirit.

Our ability to live as those *dead to sin and alive to God in Christ Jesus* comes from the same Lord Jesus Christ! It is only by the Spirit of God, at work in us by the application of faith, that we are able to present our members as instruments of righteousness rather than unrighteousness. Of course, as we continue in this life, undergoing the sanctifying work of God, we will fall from time to time into sins and into sinful patterns. When this does happen, the Word of God calls us to immediately confess and repent of our sins, in order that we may receive the forgiveness of God in Christ Jesus our Lord. Our forgiveness, as well as our ability to live more righteously, derives first and foremost from the work of the Savior, who as Paul writes, *being raised from the dead, will never die again; death no longer [having] dominion over him. For the death he died he died to sin, once for all, but the life he lives he lives to God.*

Just as our lives should be shaped by an ever-increasing conformity in righteousness to the image of Christ and an ever-increasing desire to lay aside our sinful ways, so also should our coming to the Lord's Table include an ever-increasing desire to come as those who have confessed our sins and sought to be more fully conformed to the righteousness of Christ. Just as Paul says in 1 Corinthians 11:28 then, *let [us] examine [ourselves], and so eat of the bread and drink of the cup.* Let us come to the Lord's Supper today as those who have examined ourselves according to the Word of God and by His Spirit. Let us come as those who have confessed our sins to the One who is ever and always able to forgive us our sins and to cleanse us from all unrighteousness!

PRAYER:
Our gracious and loving heavenly Father, we confess before Your throne of grace that we have yielded to temptation and are guilty of sin. We know that You have redeemed us by the blood of Jesus and justified us in Him. And yet we do continue to struggle — our inward, redeemed selves against the vestiges of sin in our flesh. Please, according to Your grace and mercy and the power of Your Spirit, strengthen us against temptation and conform us more fully day by day into the image of Jesus Christ our Savior. Please use this Lord's Supper to strengthen us for the daily battle against the sins which so easily entangle us. Feed us, we pray, upon Your matchless, transforming grace, and then send us from worship into the world that we may exalt Jesus for others to see. And it is in the precious name of Jesus that we pray. Amen.

74. Grace for the Struggles

> *So I find it to be a law that when I want to do right, evil lies close at hand. For I delight in the law of God, in my inner being, but I see in my members another law waging war against the law of my mind and making me captive to the law of sin that dwells in my members. Wretched man that I am! Who will deliver me from this body of death? Thanks be to God through Jesus Christ our Lord! So then, I myself serve the law of God with my mind, but with my flesh I serve the law of sin.*
>
> ROMANS 7:21–25

PRINCIPLE:

In this well-known text from the inspired hand of the Apostle Paul, we find described most vividly, the very crux of the believer's struggle — the ongoing inward warfare between the redeemed and transformed mind/heart and the remaining vestiges of sinful inclinations still seated in our flesh. For while we are declared justified by God and clothed in the righteousness of Christ at our conversion, the working out of that divine declaration in the actual sanctification of our entire being is ongoing — incomplete until the end of our lives, or, if sooner, the return of Christ.

Whenever we encounter Romans chapter 7, we are reminded of this struggle, which is so much a part of living the Christian life. How difficult it is for our flesh to walk in the newness of life which Christ purchased for us and the Spirit has applied to us! Yet we can fully and completely in the height of our frustration and weariness over this daily struggle, say with the Apostle Paul — *Who will deliver me from this body of death? Thanks be to God through Jesus Christ our Lord!*

We give thanks to God our Father even as we struggle. We give praise and honor and glory even in the day to day warfare between our redeemed inner man and our flesh's sinful tendencies. We do so ever and always for the work of the Lord Jesus Christ — His work in the past in dying as our substitute, His work in the present bringing about our sanctification, and His future work of our glorification.

And so when we come to the Lord's Table, we do not come as those utterly spotless and free from sin. Yet we do come as those who are redeemed in Christ and who continue to daily battle against sin. The Word of God penned by the Apostle Paul in the first letter to the church in Corinth therefore warns us to come to the Table as those who have *examined themselves*. We are to confess our sins and seek the promised forgiveness found only in Jesus. We come to the feast of the Gospel as children of God who are also constantly in need of Christ's cleansing and His grace.

> **PRAYER:**
>
> Dear King Jesus, we praise You that You have saved us from the eternal consequences of our sin. Yet we confess that for us the daily struggle continues between doing what we know from Your Word is right for a child of God and doing what our flesh strongly desires to do. We ask You as our great High Priest to help us in this daily struggle. And as we come to worship and to celebrate Communion, we ask Your Holy Spirit to convict us of any unconfessed or besetting sins and to confess and repent of them before we partake of the bread and the cup. We thank You that Your Word faithfully promises us the way of escape in times of temptation and we ask You to remind us constantly of this reassuring promise as we live by faith and not by sight in this challenging world. In Jesus' name. Amen.

75. Hope that Does Not Disappoint

And not only the creation, but we ourselves, who have the firstfruits of the Spirit, groan inwardly as we wait eagerly for adoption as sons, the redemption of our bodies. For in this hope we were saved. Now hope that is seen is not hope. For who hopes for what he sees? But if we hope for what we do not see, we wait for it with patience.

ROMANS 8:23–25

PRINCIPLE:
In this section of Romans chapter 8, the Apostle Paul reveals to us the nature of the hope we profess as believers in the Lord Jesus Christ. The great hope of the redeemed body of Christ is for the full realization of the new heaven and the new earth, inhabited by the adopted sons and daughters of God in full radiant, resurrection glory — expressed and enjoyed eternally in the presence of our Triune God.

Paul writes of this hope in a more certain way than we typically use the term today. Perhaps an expression like *certain hope* would better describe his faith-birthed and Spirit-given expectation. While we do not yet see, any more than the Apostle Paul did in his day, the full realization of the reign of the kingdom of God, nevertheless we live and work under the bright and glorious hope purchased and trail blazed by the Son of God and now under constant preparation for those of us who are heirs with Christ.

As the Apostle writes, we already enjoy the first fruits — the initial indications and proof of the gloriousness to come — through the indwelling Holy Spirit and the evidences shown forth in our redemption, transformation, and ongoing sanctification. While our bodies have not yet been renewed after the likeness of the resurrected Son, we yet have the certainty that it will one day come to pass, for we have already received the Spirit-birthed transformation of our souls and our minds.

The Lord's Supper visually displays for us the work of the Lord Jesus Christ and the hope that we profess through Him. The Spirit of God uses the elements of the Supper, the words of institution, and the participation of the covenant people of God to work in us encouragement concerning the great hope. Throughout the Word of God, from Daniel 7 to Revelation 22, the return of the Lord Jesus Christ and the fullness of His reign is associated with the fulfillment of all the hopes of the Covenant of Redemption for the elect children of God. And so, as we celebrate and as we remember the completed work of Christ on our behalf, we are also drawn by the Spirit to consider the hope of the Lord Jesus' glorious return.

May we always draw near to the Lord's Table as those who rejoice in the hope which does not disappoint. May the Spirit remind us vividly of Christ's work of redemption for us, His ongoing work of sanctification in us, and His pending return to fully restore all the creation, freed of the curse of sin, and inhabited by the resurrected saints in light! To God be all the glory, for His past, present, and future works in the creation and among His people!

PRAYER:

Heavenly Father, please help us by Your Spirit, as we receive the bread and the cup in the Supper, to recognize clearly the great hope You have given us in Jesus Christ, Your Son. We know that we already have the firstfruits of Your Holy Spirit, Who lives within us. We also know that Christ Jesus died for us, giving His body and His blood so that we might have newness of life. And yet we continue to hope and to long for that day when Jesus returns in all His glory and when we will experience the resurrection of our physical bodies, the fullness of the hope and the faith which we now profess and which is symbolized in the Lord's Supper. We give You thanks, praise, and glory, in Jesus' name. Amen.

76. If God Is for Us

> *What then shall we say to these things? If God is for us, who can be against us? He who did not spare his own Son but gave him up for us all, how will he not also with him graciously give us all things? Who shall bring any charge against God's elect? It is God who justifies. Who is to condemn? Christ Jesus is the one who died—more than that, who was raised—who is at the right hand of God, who indeed is interceding for us.*
>
> Romans 8:31–34

PRINCIPLE:

When times of great trial or perhaps great failure in our present lives seem to overwhelm us, we often fall into the trap of self-condemnation or Satan-condemnation. On the one hand we regularly face the *accuser of the brethren*, and on the other we quickly doubt our identity in Christ and accuse ourselves. Our failures to resist temptations are indeed sins before a holy God, but as His children in Christ, they do not in any way result in a change in our eternal standing before the Lord as His sons and daughters.

The believers in the church in Rome needed to hear this truth as much as we do today. In addition to dealing with their own tendencies to self-condemnation and Satan's condemnations, they also were faced with the condemnation and false charges of the culture and the governing authorities in which they lived. They were even subject to condemnation and accusation from their Jewish family and friends. The Apostle Paul, moved by the Spirit of Christ, understood these difficulties in a fallen world, faced by fallen men and women — both in the first century and in our own 21st century.

We begin sliding down a very slippery slope when we fail to remember and to live as those who have had the condemnation of God removed from us and replaced by His grace, through the work, death, and resurrection of Jesus Christ. Paul reminds us so clearly of this when he answers his own question, *Who is to condemn? Christ Jesus is the one who died—more than that, who was raised—who is at the right hand of God, who indeed is interceding for us.*

And this wonderful declaration follows the amazing revelation earlier in the text that since God did not withhold His one and only Son, but sacrificed Him to a cruel death, specifically for His elect children, He will also graciously give us all things! And the Lord Jesus Christ,

Paul reminds us, is now seated at the right hand of power beside the living God, ever and always interceding on our behalf!

In our own time in which we face economic hardships, illnesses, family struggles, difficulties resisting temptation, and ridicule for our beliefs in the popular culture — we need the application of this powerful truth of the Word of God in our lives. We need the constant reminder of our identity in Christ and of the eternal grace and generosity of God our Father in Jesus.

May the Spirit of Christ use the Lord's Supper as the Word made visible, along with this portion of Romans 8 proclaimed verbally, to powerfully remind us of who we are in Christ, and even more importantly, of Who our faithful covenant-keeping God is — the eternal Father Who has adopted us in His Son and has removed our condemnation. Since He did not withhold His one and only Son, will He not now also freely give us all things?

PRAYER:

Heavenly Father, we thank You and praise You that there is now no condemnation for those of us who by Your grace and through faith are now in Christ Jesus. We thank You that through Christ and His death and resurrection we have been justified in Your holy sight. And we thank You that these wondrous blessings are symbolized for us and brought to remembrance for us in the Lord's Supper. Holy Father, may we not simply go through the motions of eating the bread and drinking the cup. Instead, by Your Spirit, may we experience again Christ crucified and risen from the dead! May we be encouraged that we are now adopted into Your family and declared citizens of Your kingdom, through our justification in Jesus Christ, our risen Lord, in Whose name we pray. Amen.

77. He Graciously Gives Us All Things

What then shall we say to these things? If God is for us, who can be against us? He who did not spare his own Son but gave him up for us all, how will he not also with him graciously give us all things? Who shall bring any charge against God's elect? It is God who justifies. Who is to condemn? Christ Jesus is the one who died—more than that, who was raised—who is at the right hand of God, who indeed is interceding for us. Who shall separate us from the love of Christ? Shall tribulation, or distress, or persecution, or famine, or nakedness, or danger, or sword? As it is written,

"For your sake we are being killed all the day long; we are regarded as sheep to be slaughtered."

No, in all these things we are more than conquerors through him who loved us. For I am sure that neither death nor life, nor angels nor rulers, nor things present nor things to come, nor powers, nor height nor depth, nor anything else in all creation, will be able to separate us from the love of God in Christ Jesus our Lord.

ROMANS 8:31–39

PRINCIPLE:
Let us seek the face of God to strengthen us in the sure and certain, faith-birthed answer to the Apostle's question: *He who did not spare his own Son but gave him up for us all, how will he not also with him graciously give us all things?* Indeed the Lord will not withhold anything from His adopted and cherished children that is necessary for their good and their growth in grace and glory. This we know is true because God the Father has already given us the most precious and costly gift He possesses in eternity — His one and only Son, Jesus Christ our Lord.

The Lord's Supper reminds us visually, as does the proclaimed audible Word, that whatever may raise itself against us in life — whether from within us or from without us — whether *death or life, or angels or rulers, or things present or things to come, or powers, or height or depth, or anything else in all creation,* we can be absolutely certain that none of these things will ever overcome the relationship we have with God through faith in the completed, glorious work of Jesus Christ our Savior and King!

As we receive the bread and the cup, may the Holy Spirit of God refresh us and feed us through this means of His abundant grace. And may the Lord Jesus remind us anew that we are one with Him and the Father by the Spirit, and that we are one with one another as fellow heirs of God's Covenant of Redemption. There is nothing in heaven or upon earth or under the earth that can separate us from the bond of love constructed and forever sustained for us by the Father, the Son, and the Holy Spirit. *If God is for us, who can be against us?*

> **PRAYER:**
> Dear gracious and glorious eternal Father, we give You all praise and honor because in Christ Jesus You have shown Yourself to be for us. We thank You that even when everything and everyone in this present life seems to be arrayed against us, You are inseparable from us through Your eternal, covenantal love for us in Jesus Christ, Your Son, our Lord. We ask You to draw us even more closely in heart, mind, and spirit to You as we gather around Your table to receive Communion. May the simple, visible signs of the bread and cup point us ever upward in gazing upon Your smiling countenance as those who in Jesus, by Your grace, are more than conquerors! In Jesus' name we pray. Amen.

78. Nothing Can Separate Us

Who shall separate us from the love of Christ? Shall tribulation, or distress, or persecution, or famine, or nakedness, or danger, or sword? As it is written,

> *"For your sake we are being killed all the day long; we are regarded as sheep to be slaughtered."*

No, in all these things we are more than conquerors through him who loved us. For I am sure that neither death nor life, nor angels nor rulers, nor things present nor things to come, nor powers, nor height nor depth, nor anything else in all creation, will be able to separate us from the love of God in Christ Jesus our Lord.

ROMANS 8:35–39

PRINCIPLE:

With the concluding crescendo of Paul's inspired encouragement in Romans, chapter 8, we reach the gloriousness of what it means to be a redeemed child of God. No matter what challenges, trials, slanders, hardships, and adversaries may come against us, we will prevail — conquer — yes, even more than conquer — through the Lord Jesus Christ!

Only the love of Christ, fixed upon us by God's decree and implanted within us by the ministry of the Holy Spirit, ever and always accomplishes this amazing, sustaining truth. For brief and sometimes for lengthy periods of time in our lives, it seems to all outward observation and all the available evidence that we are being defeated in this fight we call the life of Christian faith. Yet in every way and in every moment, what is really taking place is our ultimate victory eternally through the sustaining and sanctifying and, one day, glorifying grace of God embodied in the love of Christ Jesus our Lord!

As we come to the Word preached and the Word made visible today, I encourage you to prayerfully consider and inwardly contemplate the great joy and the great assurance that is ours through the sacrificial and now ongoing work of the Lord Jesus Christ for you and for me. Consider how totally, completely, and powerfully the love of God in Christ is moment by moment at work within you and for you, enabling you and enabling me to achieve complete and total — eternal victory!

One of the most poignant and also beautiful aspects of the Lord's Supper is the way that it visually displays for us how the seeming defeat of the Lord Jesus Christ by the powers of darkness during His crucifixion and death, is actually used to bring about His eternal victory for all who believe. For within three days of the apparent defeat of the cross, there followed the complete and glorious victory of the resurrection and the ascension of Jesus. May we see today in the Lord's Supper the great conquering victory of Jesus, which abounds now in us by faith and is nourished within us through this marvelous means of God's grace!

PRAYER:
Heavenly Father, thank You for bringing eternal triumphal victory for us from the apparent death and defeat of Your Son Jesus on the cross of Calvary. Thank You that none of this was a surprise to You, but was all a part of Your great plan to redeem us from the ravages, the stain, and the fiery consequences of our sin. Help us by Your Holy Spirit to rest and rejoice in the saving death and the glorious, absolute victory of Jesus Christ as commune with You at the Lord's Supper. By Your great grace, encourage us that we live and walk day by day in the conquering triumph of Jesus Christ, our Lord and Savior. In His mighty, overcoming name we pray. Amen.

79. Therefore

I appeal to you therefore, brothers, by the mercies of God, to present your bodies as a living sacrifice, holy and acceptable to God, which is your spiritual worship.

ROMANS 12:1

Therefore let us be grateful for receiving a kingdom that cannot be shaken, and thus let us offer to God acceptable worship, with reverence and awe, for our God is a consuming fire.

HEBREWS 12:28–29

PRINCIPLE:
As we come to the inspired and holy Word of God and the Word of God made visible through the Lord's Supper, let's reflect upon the related verses above from Romans and Hebrews.

In the first place, both texts urge us as the redeemed people of God to engage in worship. And in the second place, both texts give us reasons why we are called to worship as the people of God. In Romans 12 the mercies of God to us in the work of Christ Jesus are in view. In Hebrews 12, the victorious kingdom of God we have received, and the Lord's holiness are in view.

Yet while both texts exhort us to worship the Lord, the Apostle Paul in Romans is unmistakably clear that all of our lives as the redeemed in Christ are to be lived out as living sacrifices of acceptable worship to God.

Based upon this truth, we can say that our formal, covenantal, corporate worship as the people of God on the Lord's Day is interconnected with our daily image-bearing of Christ as we fulfill our callings, interact with family, neighbors, friends, or co-workers, and minister to one another.

In effect, our regular congregational Sunday morning worship gatherings are a time for us to be reinvigorated and further equipped to live worshipful lives throughout the other six days of the week! Therefore, our sitting under the Word declared and the Word made visible on Sunday are precisely the spiritual nourishment we need to propel us forward for God's kingdom in the remainder of each new week.

May the Lord by His Holy Spirit, empower and equip you through the reading and preaching of the Word and through your participation in the Lord's Supper, to live lives of worship to God in

Christ each and every day. May the Lord bless each one of you in each new week our Father graciously gives to us!

> **PRAYER:**
>
> Our great God and Father, we thank You for Your means of grace in the prayers, preaching, and partaking in the Lord's Supper during our seasons of kingdom worship. We praise You for using our Sabbath worship, including the Sacraments, as a means to encourage, equip, and empower us to serve You and to exalt King Jesus during the unfolding days of every new week. Holy Father, by Your eternal Spirit, help us to offer both acceptable Lord's Day worship which glorifies You, and acceptable spiritual worship each and every day in ministering Christ to others. May we not be transformed by the world in which we live, but instead may we bring the power of the Gospel to transform the world and bring it under the dominion of Jesus and His kingdom. In Jesus' name we pray. Amen.

80. One in Christ Jesus

For as in one body we have many members, and the members do not all have the same function, so we, though many, are one body in Christ, and individually members one of another. Having gifts that differ according to the grace given to us, let us use them: if prophecy, in proportion to our faith; if service, in our serving; the one who teaches, in his teaching; the one who exhorts, in his exhortation; the one who contributes, in generosity; the one who leads, with zeal; the one who does acts of mercy, with cheerfulness.

ROMANS 12:4–8

PRINCIPLE:
The Apostle Paul reveals to us in Romans 12 and in 1 Corinthians 12 the absolute necessity for God's people to exercise their gifts and talents for the sake of Christ's kingdom. Each redeemed child of God has particular talents, or sets of gifts and talents, which are essential for wider body life. In fact, the Lord gave them uniquely to each one of us in various mixtures and degrees specifically so that we may then contribute these gifts and talents to build up the other people of God within the church.

Now Paul also emphasizes that while the gifts and talents given to each believer vary widely, we are all nevertheless one body in Jesus Christ. Just as he writes in Romans 12:4: *For as in one body we have many members, and the members do not all have the same function, so we, though many, are one body in Christ, and individually members one of another.* So the Apostle both exhorts us to celebrate the diversity of God's good gifts among His people, and the unity we enjoy together as members of the one body of Christ — the Church. Paul repeats this theme again in his first epistle to the Corinthians. And this principle, revealed by God, is one that we very much need to learn and apply if we are to be a healthy, biblically-based church.

Just as the written Word of God preached orally today heightens our awareness of both the diversity and unity of the body of Christ, so also the Sacrament of the Lord's Supper does much the same thing using visual and tactile communication. As the Holy Spirit does His unique and powerful work in each of us during the Supper, we are both reminded of our own individual salvation in Christ and our membership in His family, as well as our being *members one of another.* Our redemption is connected through Christ and the Spirit with the salvation of all those who were, who are now, and who one day will be saved!

And thus the Lord's Supper serves to underline the importance for us of recognizing our relationship with other believers within our local congregation and throughout the world, through the redeeming graces we all share in Jesus. As we eat of the bread and recall Jesus carrying away our sins up onto the cross upon His sinless shoulders, we should also remember that God has saved others among us, bearing away their sins just as He once did ours. And we also drink together from the cup, reminded of the shed blood of the Son of God, willingly spilt in order to wash away our sins as believers in Him!

PRAYER:

Our gracious and loving heavenly Father, by Your Spirit and through our Lord Jesus Christ, sustain us and keep us as one unified body of Christ. Lead each one of us as members of one another to share Your good gifts and graces and to support one another in the love of Christ. May Your Holy Spirit bless our celebration together of the Lord's Supper. May we come without bitterness or division or offense toward one another, but instead with awareness that we all adopted brothers and sisters in Christ Jesus, made Your eternal children through the body and blood of Christ, our Lord. We give You all thanks, and honor, and praise. In Jesus' name. Amen.

81. Sexual Sin and the Supper

> *The body is not meant for sexual immorality, but for the Lord, and the Lord for the body. And God raised the Lord and will also raise us up by his power. Do you not know that your bodies are members of Christ? Shall I then take the members of Christ and make them members of a prostitute? Never! Or do you not know that he who is joined with a prostitute becomes one body with her? For, as it is written, "The two will become one flesh." But he who is joined to the Lord becomes one spirit with him. Flee from sexual immorality. Every other sin a person commits is outside the body, but the sexually immoral person sins against his own body. Or do you not know that your body is a temple of the Holy Spirit within you, whom you have from God? You are not your own, for you were bought with a price. So glorify God in your body.*
>
> 1 Corinthians 6:13b–20

PRINCIPLE:

As a believer in Christ, my body has been transformed into a temple in which the Holy Spirit of God makes his dwelling. I am a part of the covenant people and the body of Christ my Savior. Therefore, the life I live in this world cannot be separated from the Spirit of Christ. How I live my life also affects other members of Christ's body. When I commit sexual sins of any kind, whether lustful thoughts, viewing printed, cable, or on-line pornography, self-stimulation, premarital or extramarital sex, or paying someone for sex — as the Apostle Paul describes in this passage — I am harming my own body, harming the corporate body of Christ, and sinning against the perfectly Holy Spirit of God who lives within me. Fellowship with the Spirit of God and with other believers is impaired when I engage in this sinful activity which is so widely encouraged in today's culture. As I approach the celebration of the Lord's Supper, I must deal with this aspect of my sinfulness.

All of us have a responsibility and an important role to play as members of the corporate body of Christ as well. When we come to the Table we come as part of a larger family redeemed in Christ. Our fellowship with each other as children of God, as well as our fellowship around the Table with Christ, is impacted by the sexual faithfulness we practice in our daily lives — both inwardly and outwardly.

PRAYER:

My gracious and loving Heavenly Father, Holy God and giver of the Spirit of Christ, I know you have placed your Holy Spirit within me through the completed work and promise of Christ. Thank you for his marvelous presence and for the daily transformation He is working in me. And yet as I kneel in your presence gracious Father, I am also reminded that You are zealous for my body, Your temple, and that You are perfectly holy. My life just doesn't measure up to Your perfect standard. As I seek Your face today and reflect upon Your Word, I am convicted of my deep longings to satisfy my strong sexual desires in ways which are selfish, destructive to my body and to others, and offensive to You.

Forgive me Father, through the cleansing blood of Jesus Christ my Savior! Enable me by the daily work and presence of Your Holy Spirit to walk more and more in newness of life, conformed more fully to the image of Jesus. Help me — remind me — convict me when lustful thoughts and images enter into my heart and my mind, that You are within me and that I am no longer my own to pursue my own selfish desires. Grant that I may glorify You with all my body — my heart, my mind, and all that I am. Prepare me, even now, as a member of the body of Christ, a temple of Your Holy presence and glory, for table fellowship with Jesus and with my brothers and sisters, adopted together into Your family. I know that I will never be able to do this, or even desire to do this, apart from Your powerful working and enabling strength and grace, through Jesus Christ Your Son, in whose name I pray. Amen.

82. Remembrance, Presence, and Anticipation through the Supper

For I received from the Lord what I also delivered to you, that the Lord Jesus on the night when he was betrayed took bread, and when he had given thanks, he broke it, and said, "This is my body which is for you. Do this in remembrance of me." In the same way also he took the cup, after supper, saying, "This cup is the new covenant in my blood. Do this, as often as you drink it, in remembrance of me." For as often as you eat this bread and drink the cup, you proclaim the Lord's death until he comes.
1 CORINTHIANS 11:23–26

PRINCIPLE:
The Apostle Paul provides an account for us of Jesus' words at the institution of the Supper which agrees with the Gospel writers' accounts and also provides some additional information. The words Paul received from the Lord Jesus and passed on to the Corinthians emphasize three concepts which are important for our own observances of Communion today.

The first principle is that of representation or symbolic correspondence between the elements and the person and work of Jesus. As in the Gospel accounts, the bread serves to represent Jesus' body, *which is for you*. Likewise, the cup represents Jesus' poured out blood, *the new covenant*. These simple elements are used by the Spirit to convey to us the benefits and blessings of Jesus' sin-bearing yet sinless body and His atoning blood.

The second principle brought to light on the Supper in 1 Corinthians 11 is that of remembrance. This concept is emphasized in this passage by its inclusion within both statements concerning the elements. Both the bread and the cup include the words, *Do this... in remembrance of me*. And so Jesus intends that we be reminded of His completed work, suffering and dying in our place, whenever we gather together to receive the Lord's Supper.

Finally, the third principle, which appears only in this passage and not in the Gospel record, is the concept of anticipation. Our celebration of Communion brings together for us the past, the present, and the future. The Lord's Supper is indeed a remembrance or memorial, bringing to mind and heart the completed work of Christ.

And it serves to celebrate Jesus' accepted work and present reign at the Father's right hand, through which we presently — by the Holy Spirit — have fellowship with Him. Yet it also includes a future aspect. For as we celebrate the Lord's Supper, we have hopeful anticipation of our Savior's return in glory.

May the Lord Jesus Christ, through the powerful operation of His Spirit within and among us, vividly display in our hearts and our minds these three aspects of His sacrificial love. No wonder that some congregations throughout the history of the Church have also referred to the Lord's Supper as a *Love Feast!*

PRAYER:

Lord Jesus, we thank You that on that last night with Your disciples, before You were betrayed, that You celebrated a last Passover meal with them. We thank You that during this Last Supper You declared a new Passover — the Lord's Supper, and that You took the unleavened bread of the Passover and declared it to represent Your sinless body, given for us. We also praise You for taking the cup of blessing and declaring it to symbolize the sin-cleansing blood You were about to shed to seal the new covenant for our redemption. As we come to this new Passover feast — this Communion celebration, may all of the richness of these symbols and the eternal truths to which they point us be made even more powerful in sanctifying us and equipping us spiritually to declare Your Gospel to so many others who need to hear it. In Your name we pray. Amen.

83. The Lord's Supper: A Weekly Memorial Day

For as often as you eat this bread and drink the cup, you proclaim the Lord's death until he comes.

1 CORINTHIANS 11:26

PRINCIPLE:

On a designated day each year, millions of Americans observe a day of remembrance, both for those men and women who have died in military service to our nation, and in addition, for many other family members who through death are now separated from us in this present life. I remember well, as a boy, going to the family cemetery with my parents and placing American flags on my ancestors' graves and simple flower arrangements on grandparents' and great-grandparents' markers. I also remember patriotic services and parades, designed to remember those who paid the ultimate price for the freedom we now enjoy.

While there are many practicing believers who participate in our nation's annual Memorial Day observances, there are others who were not raised in this practice or who simply choose to focus on the present spiritual location of their loved ones, rather than their current physical resting place. It is my view that both practices are useful, and quite frankly serve to benefit in various ways — not those who have died — but those of us who remain in this present life.

Having said all of this, I want to be clear that there is another form of Memorial Day that every believing Christian is instructed to observe. In fact, the Bible exhorts us to observe this service of remembrance often. Of course, what I am referring to is the Lord's Supper, which some congregations celebrate quarterly, some monthly, and some weekly.

As we gather for each Communion, we gather around the Lord's Table in order to proclaim the Lord Jesus' death *until he comes*. Our congregational proclamation through Communion serves to visually declare or *preach* the atoning death and completed work of Jesus our Savior. Our Lord Himself instructed His disciples to do this very thing in *remembrance of me* (see Luke 22:19; 1 Corinthians 11:24, 25). And so for those of us who believe in Jesus Christ, there are always to be covenant family *memorial* or *remembrance* days, in which we both remember what the Son of God did in dying in our place, and celebrating our new, redeemed identities as adopted children of God through Christ. Through Jesus' servant sacrifice we have been delivered from eternal death and slavery to sin, and given everlasting life with freedom in Him.

In addition, our regular Lord's Supper memorial day celebrations serve to build up within us an expectation of King Jesus' glorious return. On that majestic and joyous day, those of us who have trusted in Him will be reunited with our believing loved ones and all the saints of God. Our memorial days and remembrance meals will be replaced on that day by the marriage supper of the Lamb, the great banquet celebrating the final consummation of Christ's kingdom (Revelation 19:6–9).

PRAYER:

Lord Jesus, we come into Your presence now to celebrate the Supper that You have instructed us to keep as a perpetual memorial of what You did to save us from sin and give to us eternal life. Like the Passover meal of old, this Gospel Feast proclaims the Father's mighty deliverance of His people through the blood of the Passover Lamb. You, Lord Jesus, are the ultimate fulfillment of God's mighty deliverance as the Lamb who takes away the sin of the world. We praise You, King Jesus for giving Your precious, sinless life as a ransom for many. We rejoice and we remember the salvation You worked for us. We see it symbolized in the bread and in the cup that we share. We hear it in the words of institution. We touch and we taste it represented in the simple elements. Every time we do this, Lord Jesus, we indeed proclaim anew Your sacrificial death, until You come again for the marriage supper of the Lamb. Oh, Lord Jesus, how we long for the sweetness and the completeness we will know when You return in glory. Encourage us with that blessed hope we pray, by the Holy Spirit, as we see You spiritually in this Sacrament. In Your mighty name we pray. Amen.

84. The Cheerful Giver, the One Who Gave Everything, and the Supper

> *The point is this: whoever sows sparingly will also reap sparingly, and whoever sows bountifully will also reap bountifully. Each one must give as he has made up his mind, not reluctantly or under compulsion, for God loves a cheerful giver. And God is able to make all grace abound to you, so that having all sufficiency in all things at all times, you may abound in every good work. As it is written, "He has distributed freely, he has given to the poor; his righteousness endures forever." He who supplies seed to the sower and bread for food will supply and multiply your seed for sowing and increase the harvest of your righteousness. You will be enriched in every way for all your generosity, which through us will produce thanksgiving to God. For the ministry of this service is not only supplying the needs of the saints, but is also overflowing in many thanksgivings to God. By their approval of this service, they will glorify God because of your submission flowing from your confession of the gospel of Christ, and the generosity of your contribution for them and for all others, while they long for you and pray for you, because of the surpassing grace of God upon you. Thanks be to God for his inexpressible gift!*
>
> 2 Corinthians 9:6–15

PRINCIPLE:

With direct exhortations such as the Apostle Paul's in 2 Corinthians 9, and with lived-out examples, the Holy Scriptures urge upon believers the importance of material giving to God's kingdom people and purposes. The Old Testament prophet Malachi is well known for his rebuke of the people of God in his own time for their *robbing of God* in their inadequate tithes and offerings. And the tendency to withhold giving to God's visible institutions is not limited to Malachi's day. Believers in our day battle constantly against the temptation to put our own desires in finances ahead of the Lord's purposes and His priorities for the means He has placed in our trust to faithfully steward.

How do we overcome our fallen tendency to selfishness when it comes to financial resources? I believe we will never overcome it through willpower alone, through the guilt inducing haranguing of ministers, or with the guidance of all the self-help financial freedom gurus. We will only arrive at being a truly cheerful giver through the transforming work of Jesus Christ within our hearts and our lives. It is only when the Spirit of God enables us to grasp something of the selfless, priceless gift that we have received from Christ, that we are truly enabled to be cheerful givers. The Apostle Paul declares Jesus' work as the basis for Christian giving when he writes to the Corinthians that their service in this way was the result of their submission *flowing from their confession of the Gospel of Christ*, and the resulting *generosity of their contribution for them and for all others*.

The Bible teaches us that *we love because he [God] first loved us*. And it is certainly just as true that we give to God and to others because Jesus first gave to us. He gave to the uttermost, shedding His blood and giving His very life to that we who believe in Him may now live and live forevermore! Christ's one-time sacrificial gift blesses us eternally with gifts and graces beyond measure, and spiritual and physical provisions we can never assign a value. All of this is a part of what is represented for us in the bread and the cup of the Lord's Supper. May our remembrance around the Table, of Christ's measureless gift to us, and His ongoing gracious provisions, work in us cheerfulness and generosity in kingdom giving.

PRAYER:
Heavenly Father, we pray that You will transform us into truly cheerful givers. We ask You to remind us by Your Spirit through the Lord's Supper of just how very much You have loved us and abundantly given us everything that we need in this life and in eternity to come. Help us see Christ's greatest gift of love when we receive the bread and drink from the cup, which so simply and beautifully remind us of Jesus' body and blood, given selflessly for us. May Your matchless grace and Christ's priceless sacrifice for our salvation continually transform how we think and how we act when it comes to kingdom giving — giving to Your Body the Church or giving to others in need. As we do so in seeking to image Jesus, may our kingdom giving abound in thanksgivings to You and to Jesus Christ our Lord and Savior, in Whose name we pray. Amen.

85. Rich in Mercy

> *But God, being rich in mercy, because of the great love with which he loved us, even when we were dead in our trespasses, made us alive together with Christ — by grace you have been saved — and raised us up with him and seated us with him in the heavenly places in Christ Jesus, so that in the coming ages he might show the immeasurable riches of his grace in kindness toward us in Christ Jesus.*
>
> Ephesians 2:4–7

PRINCIPLE:

The Apostle Paul was mightily used by the Spirit of God to declare the Lord's great love and grace toward everyone whom He has *made alive together with Christ.* This portion of Paul's letter to the believers in Ephesus is full of the language of mercy, love, grace, and kindness. All of these marvelous attributes of Yahweh are lavished richly upon every chosen and redeemed child of God in Christ Jesus His Son!

As if to underline this eternal reality more fully, the Apostle writes not only in general terms of God's grace and blessings for His chosen children, but also specifically of the way in which God's grace so closely connects us with Jesus Himself. Paul reveals that just as we are saved from our trespasses and sins by Jesus' atoning death on the cross, so also we are raised up with the Lord Jesus in His resurrection glory and in newness of life, and we are further seated with God in the heavenly places in Christ! All of this was accomplished according to the redemptive plan of the God the Father, God the Son, and God the Holy Spirit, so that in the new heaven and new earth — fully realized at Jesus' return — God *might show the immeasurable riches of his grace in kindness toward us in Christ Jesus!*

What an incredible, unfathomable, eternal inheritance we have as believers in Jesus Christ! And yet Paul tells us that we do not gain all of these divine treasures because of anything that we have done to earn them, or even anything we do to continue to keep them. Rather, we are the heirs of all these things in Christ Jesus, according to God's grace alone. It is God's particular grace fixed upon us by means of the free gift of faith that enables us to live in union with Christ and enjoy God's immense blessings.

God's grace toward the men and women He has made in His own image is described in Scripture as taking two forms. There is His common grace — that is, His kindness to all of the creation and all of mankind. Then there is His particular grace, which I believe includes both saving grace and sustaining grace. As believers in Jesus, saved according to God's grace, the Lord continues to provide for us by means of His sustaining grace. We receive God's sustaining grace by the means He has given to us: proclamation of the Word, prayer, and the Sacraments.

It is therefore extremely beneficial for you, in seeking to grow in the practice of your faith and in relationship with God in Christ, that you appropriate the means of grace the Lord has provided for you. Please take the opportunity each Lord's Day to ask Him to feed you richly, deeply, lavishly upon His sustaining grace through the preaching, prayers, and the celebration of the Lord's Supper.

PRAYER:

Dear heavenly Father, we praise You for the riches of Your mercy and grace to us in Christ Jesus our Lord. We thank You that by faith You have united us with Christ Jesus in His atoning death. Even more so You have also united us to Jesus in His resurrection glory and in His ascension to the heavenly places at Your right hand of power. We praise You for Your lavish blessings to us through Jesus Your Son. Please continue to lavish upon us the riches of Your grace as we come before You to receive the Lord's Supper. May the Spirit of Christ feed us and fill us in overflowing proportions with the benefits of what Christ Jesus has done and continued to do for all who believe in His name. In Jesus' name we pray. Amen.

86. The Body of Christ: Diverse and Unified

But grace was given to each one of us according to the measure of Christ's gift. Therefore it says, "When he ascended on high he led a host of captives, and he gave gifts to men." ... And he gave the apostles, the prophets, the evangelists, the shepherds and teachers, to equip the saints for the work of ministry, for building up the body of Christ, until we all attain to the unity of the faith and of the knowledge of the Son of God, to mature manhood, to the measure of the stature of the fullness of Christ, so that we may no longer be children, tossed to and fro by the waves and carried about by every wind of doctrine, by human cunning, by craftiness in deceitful schemes. Rather, speaking the truth in love, we are to grow up in every way into him who is the head, into Christ, from whom the whole body, joined and held together by every joint with which it is equipped, when each part is working properly, makes the body grow so that it builds itself up in love.

EPHESIANS 4:7–8, 11–16

PRINCIPLE:
The Lord Jesus Christ designed the Church to display both amazing diversity and marvelous unity at the very same time. This great truth of God's kingdom is described for us here in Paul's letter to the believers of the Ephesian congregation in chapter 4. Paul is given the Spirit-inspired vision of the Lord Jesus Christ's ascension into heaven and the implications of that for those who believe in Him.

Paul writes that like the mightiest of conquerors the resurrected Lord Jesus led in triumph *a host of captives*, while simultaneously giving great gifts to His kingdom people. The Apostle reveals that among these gifts are those called to be *apostles, prophets, evangelists, shepherds and teachers*. And Jesus gave these people, with their special equipping and kingdom tasks to perform, as gifts for the building up of the people of God, the Church.

This diversity of gifts and callings, represented by the list Paul gives us in this passage, is carefully designed and granted to His Church in order that all of us who believe may *attain to the unity of the faith and of the knowledge of the Son of God*, to Christian maturity, and to the measure of the fullness of Christ. As we are equipped by those so-called, we will grow up into Christ, into a whole body joined together, growing so that we are built up in the love of God.

Just as Christ works among His people in the Church, utilizing diversity to achieve unity, so also the Lord's Supper displays for us both the diversity and the unity of the body of Christ as the redeemed family of God. Though there are as many giftings and callings in our local congregation as there are brothers and sisters present, at the same time we are unified as one body in Christ. We all share in the same Spirit, and in *one Lord, one faith, one baptism, one hope, one God and Father of all, who is in all and through all* (Ephesians 4:5–6). As participants around His table, we are one in the Lord Jesus Christ, all saved through His marvelous grace!

PRAYER:

Dear Lord Jesus, You are the head of God's Church and so You are the head of our local congregation. We praise You for Your good gifts to our local body of men and women who live to serve one another. We praise You for raising up elders and deacons, for Sunday school teachers and nursery workers, for every sort of ministry calling which is filled by our brothers and sisters in Christ. We praise You for our pastors and assistant pastors and for those who volunteer as ushers and greeters. We thank You for those who lead worship and those who collect the offering. We thank You for those who are always serving quietly, behind the scenes, and who never seek the recognition of men. We also thank You that You use these diversities of gifts and callings to further the unity of the Body of Christ, the Church, in preparing it as Your Bride for the day of Your glorious return. Now we ask that You would anoint us afresh with the Holy Spirit as we celebrate Communion together. May the Spirit work in our hearts, our minds, and our lives as we share in the Supper, such that we truly love You and in the same manner truly love one another as well. In Your saving name we pray. Amen.

87. Imitators of God

Therefore be imitators of God as beloved children. And walk in love, as Christ loved us and gave himself up for us, a fragrant offering and sacrifice to God.

Ephesians 5:1–2

PRINCIPLE:
Just as healthy children learn and grow after the influence, character, and teaching of their parents, so we also as children of God in Christ should reflect the character of the Lord. The primary characteristic of this imaging of God we are exhorted to exhibit is Spirit-birthed, unselfish love. This is because selfless love, guided by the Father's will, always marked the ministry of the Lord Jesus Christ. It also marks the character of God — Father, Son, and Holy Spirit — in dealing with us through election, redemption, regeneration, and ongoing sanctification.

Imaging the selfless, Spirit-birthed love of Christ in our daily walk as Christians will sometimes lead to marked periods of suffering and sacrifice — sacrifice we may experience in trials, deprivations, and pain. Yet the Apostle Paul is not only referring to those intense times of self-denial or extreme testing. He is referring to an all-of-life practice of our believing faith in which our thoughts, words, and actions each and every day — in times both of blessing and times of tribulation — glorify God in Christ. As we do this, we testify to the transforming power of the Gospel of Jesus, not only in our lives, but also as it is offered by us to those who see our testimony on a daily basis.

The Lord's Supper testifies to us, each time that we receive it by faith, about the fragrant offering and sacrifice that Jesus made on our behalf to God our Father. Through His atoning death and glorious resurrection we are delivered from sin and from God's fierce and holy wrath. Jesus is indeed for us *the Lamb of God who takes away the sin of the world*. The Supper also reminds us that since we have received God's forgiveness and blessing in Jesus, we are now God's adopted children and co-heirs with the Lord Jesus. Therefore the Sacrament signifies for us and reminds us of our union and communion with God our Father. We now have a seat at God's table of celebration and deliverance — thanks to Christ our Savior!

I encourage you to always draw near to the Lord's Supper in the full assurance of the faith which God has birthed in your hearts and minds by the powerful working of the Spirit of Christ. Come and be nourished by God's means of grace. Come and be refreshed, and also reminded of what Christ has done for you. Come and be further equipped and encouraged to fulfill what the Apostle Paul exhorted the believers in Ephesus to do — *to walk in love, as Christ loved us and gave himself up for us, a fragrant offering and sacrifice to God.*

> **PRAYER:**
> Heavenly Father, by Your Holy Spirit transform us so that we walk more fully according to the love of Jesus Christ, Who loved us and gave Himself up for us. As He was a fragrant offering and sacrifice to You for our sakes, may we now walk in Jesus' footsteps of love and offer ourselves by faith daily as an offering and sacrifice to Your glory and honor. Father, we know that we can never do this in our own strength. Yet we know that we can do this by Your powerful grace. We ask You now to feed us lavishly upon Your grace by the Spirit and according to faith as we partake of the bread and the cup together as Your adopted children in Christ. May we see with spiritual eyes even more clearly the great love of Jesus and His selfless sacrifice for our eternal salvation. In all of these things, heavenly Father, we give You the praise and the glory in Jesus' name. Amen.

88. The Mind of Christ

Have this mind among yourselves, which is yours in Christ Jesus, who, though he was in the form of God, did not count equality with God a thing to be grasped, but made himself nothing, taking the form of a servant, being born in the likeness of men. And being found in human form, he humbled himself by becoming obedient to the point of death, even death on a cross. Therefore God has highly exalted him and bestowed on him the name that is above every name, so that at the name of Jesus every knee should bow, in heaven and on earth and under the earth, and every tongue confess that Jesus Christ is Lord, to the glory of God the Father.

PHILIPPIANS 2:5–10

PRINCIPLE:

The Christmas season is a wonderful time to remind our children and our grandchildren (and for some of you, great-grandchildren) just what God gave us when He sent His Son Jesus some two thousand years ago into a world desperately in need of a Savior. For many centuries God had promised His people through patriarchs, kings, and prophets that He would send them a Deliverer — a Messiah. And then one night in the Judean countryside in the little town of Bethlehem the promised Savior was born, Jesus Christ the Lord.

The Apostle Paul, while writing to the church in Philippi, understood so very personally how much Jesus had done so that he could have eternal life. He knew how Jesus had come, identified with us, suffered, died, then rose again and ascended into heaven. But the Spirit of God also gave Paul the insight to understand the sacrifice Jesus made BEFORE his sacrifice on the cross. Paul reveals in Philippians 2 that Jesus' sacrifice of love for us began well before He was arrested, tried, and put to death in Calvary. Christ's sacrifice began in the heavenly realm, in the gloriousness of God's throne chamber, when Jesus agreed with His Father that He would lay aside His exalted status, and as Paul writes, *made himself nothing, taking the form of a servant, being born in the likeness of men.*

"What wondrous love is this, O my soul, O my soul," as the American folk hymn of 1835 goes, "that caused the Lord of bliss to bear the dreadful curse for my soul, for my soul!" And indeed the greatest gift of love ever given, the most perfect act of selflessness and humility, was this humbling of Himself that Christ willingly endured so that we would become children of God and co-heirs with Him in glory. Jesus' humbling pathway began in the glories of God the Father's presence, led to His incarnation and humble birth to a poor couple in a small town, continued to His itinerant preaching ministry, reached its fullness in His betrayal, afflictions, and cruel death. And yet with His triumphant resurrection to His humility was added anew His glorious exaltation. As Paul writes, *Therefore God has highly exalted him and bestowed on him the name that is above every name, so that at the name of Jesus every knee should bow, in heaven and on earth and under the earth, and every tongue confess that Jesus Christ is Lord, to the glory of God the Father.*

As we gather with our families and friends during the Christmas season, may we do so not only in celebration of the first coming of Jesus Christ as a small babe crying in a manger. May we also celebrate what that birth meant and continues to mean today. And may we remember what Jesus came to do and actually accomplished — offering Himself as a perfect and living sacrifice in our place, so that we by faith receive the free gift of eternal life through Him. May our worship in song, in prayer, in Word, and in the Sacrament, guide us in celebrating this greatest of all gifts!

PRAYER:
Lord Jesus, we thank You that You did not consider the glories You enjoyed with the Father something to be tightly grasped, but instead made Yourself nothing and took the form of a servant — a servant whose purpose was to fulfill the Father's perfect Law and then die as our substitute. We praise our heavenly Father that He did not leave You in that borrowed tomb, but instead raised You gloriously, triumphantly from the dead. We bow our knees before You and we joyfully confess with our tongues that You are Lord, to the glory of God our Father. By the Spirit and by faith may we now keep this Gospel Feast in such a way that this great work of eternal redemption You have accomplished will be proclaimed and also lived out in our lives for all to see. In Jesus' name we pray. Amen.

89. Jesus, the Radiance of the Glory of God

> *Long ago, at many times and in many ways, God spoke to our fathers by the prophets, but in these last days he has spoken to us by his Son, whom he appointed the heir of all things, through whom also he created the world. He is the radiance of the glory of God and the exact imprint of his nature, and he upholds the universe by the word of his power. After making purification for sins, he sat down at the right hand of the Majesty on high, having become as much superior to angels as the name he has inherited is more excellent than theirs.*
>
> HEBREWS 1:1–4

PRINCIPLE:
According to the inspired author of Hebrews, and from what we know of the teachings of the other books of the New Testament, the Lord Jesus Christ represents the ultimate revelation of God. Jesus' teachings, miracles, and prophetic declarations more fully testified of God the Father and His plan for redeeming the creation than even the great prophets of old. Jesus is also the ultimate revelation of God because He is God's Word made flesh. He truly is *the exact imprint* of God the Father's divine nature, and in Jesus we are able to glimpse *the radiance of the glory of God* as well.

God also spoke to us by His Son Jesus through His suffering, His cross, and through His empty tomb. In all of these things that Jesus' accomplished to save us from eternal damnation because of our sin, He also declared to us God the Father's will — His accomplished Covenant of Redemption, ransoming a people for Himself from every tribe, and nation, and people, and language from all of the earth. As believers in Jesus Christ, you and I have truly seen God. It is not that we have gazed into the immediate presence of the face of our holy God, seated upon His lofty throne, as Moses had desired to do. But rather, that as we come to know Jesus, by the Spirit and by faith, through His Word, we also come to know the eternal, holy Father as well. Jesus, as God's Son, has indeed made the Father known. And it is possible for us to draw near to God the Father through Christ Jesus His Son because Jesus made purification for our sins, sealing God's covenant to redeem us with His own precious blood.

All of this is depicted for us in some way in the Sacrament of the Lord's Supper. The words of institution declare that every time we eat of the bread and drink of the cup, *we proclaim the Lord's death until he comes* (1 Corinthians 11:26). Thus Communion speaks to us, through the words and through the symbols of the bread and the cup, concerning God's own Son, Jesus Christ, as the ultimate revealer of God and the ultimate instrument for fulfilling His plan of eternal redemption for all whom He has chosen — all who call on His name by faith.

> **PRAYER:**
>
> Our gracious and loving heavenly Father, please use the Lord's Supper to reveal Yourself more fully to us through Jesus, by Your Spirit, as the words of institution are spoken, as the bread of His body is broken, and as the cup is offered as a token of Jesus' shed blood. May we more fully see You as we remember the Lord Jesus, Your one and only Son. May the Son and the Spirit together bear witness through the Supper of Your radiant glory, Your redeeming love, and Your covenantal faithfulness to Your chosen people. In Jesus' name we pray. Amen.

90. There Remains a Sabbath Rest

For if Joshua had given them rest, God would not have spoken of another day later on. So then, there remains a Sabbath rest for the people of God, for whoever has entered God's rest has also rested from his works as God did from his.

HEBREWS 4:8 – 10

PRINCIPLE:
Ever since the first week of the creation, God has established a cycle of six days of work, followed by one day of rest and of worship. This is the rhythm which marks the progress of our lives. Of course, this rhythm is lost on those who do not believe in the God of the Bible or in Jesus Christ, His Son. Yet the Lord also uses the concept of Sabbath rest as a term for the eternal peace and restoration of the creation which He will bring about when Jesus returns in glory. And Christ spoke about Himself as a place of rest for those who were weary and heavy laden in this life.

The author of Hebrews was inspired to write his book based upon the relationship between the working of God in the Old Testament era before Christ's coming and His working in the new era through Christ. In doing this, Hebrews often presents believers in Jesus as being on the wilderness road between their salvation from slavery to sin and their final entrance into God's Promised Land. Like the tribes of the Hebrews of old, believers today have been delivered, but they continue to face the trials and challenges of this present world and are tempted to grumble, to complain, to doubt, and even to test the God of their salvation.

In Hebrews 3–4, the Lord warns His people not to reject God as many of the people in the wilderness had done and not to harden their hearts — not to continually put God to the test. But instead, to constantly seek that rest by faith which God has promised. For all who persevere by faith in Jesus will enter that Sabbath rest of God when they enter into glory at the end of their journey of faith in this life.

We in the church of Jesus Christ continue to observe the weekly Sabbath rest which God ordained at the beginning of His creation, only changing the day of rest from the seventh day to the first day, in light of the resurrection day of our Lord Jesus. Our weekly Sabbaths remind us that we do find even in this life spiritual rest in Christ. And these Sundays of worship and rest also point forward to God's promised

Sabbath rest for all who finish the race of faith, who complete their wilderness journey and arrive at the Promised Land.

As we gather weekly for Sabbath worship, churches all over the world also celebrate the Lord's Supper, which serves to remind us that it is only because of Christ that we enjoy spiritual rest in this present life from our many burdens, and that it is only because of Christ that we have a sure and certain hope that by faith we will one day enter God's eternal Sabbath rest. Hebrews 4 exhorts us to strive to enter that rest and the Lord's Supper is one of the ways in which God gives us the grace and strength to continue along our path in this life striving to reach His promised rest in glory.

PRAYER:

Dear heavenly Father, thank You for helping us to understand through our Sabbath days in this life, that You have prepared seasons of rest for us. We praise You for our weekly Sundays in worship and in physical rest. We praise You especially that Your Son Jesus is our daily refuge of Sabbath rest. And we honor You for creating for us a future place of eternal Sabbath rest, which we may enter by finishing our journey of faith in this life, by striving to reach it in Christ Jesus our Lord. Help us along the way to our place of eternal Sabbath rest by feeding us upon Your grace through the Lord's Supper, as well as through prayer and the Word faithfully preached. May we find in You our weekly Sabbath rest. May we daily rest in Christ. And by Your Spirit and Your grace may we one day enter Your Sabbath rest, which remains for the people of God. In Jesus, our place of rest, we pray. Amen.

91. Jesus' Purifying Blood, Servanthood, and the Supper

For if the sprinkling of defiled persons with the blood of goats and bulls and with the ashes of a heifer sanctifies for the purification of the flesh, how much more will the blood of Christ, who through the eternal Spirit offered himself without blemish to God, purify our conscience from dead works to serve the living God.

Hebrews 9:13–14

PRINCIPLE:
The author of the letter to the Hebrews was moved by God to demonstrate that all the shadows, types, and principles displayed in the Old Testament sacrificial system were fulfilled once and for all eternity in the one-time sacrifice of Jesus Christ. Indeed, the shed of blood of Jesus, so powerfully represented in the cup at the Lord's Table through the working of the Holy Spirit, is the means by which our consciences have been purified from dead works — as Hebrews so powerfully declares.

We understand by faith that Jesus' atoning death and His precious spilt blood have removed the guilt and weight of our sins. Christ bore all our defiling transgressions and disobedience upon His sinless shoulders the hours He hung on that cross as our substitute. What we often may not fully understand or may simply forget, however, is the second transforming truth declared in this passage about what the blood of Christ accomplished. In purifying us as God's elect children through His shed blood, Jesus *also called and consecrated us in kingdom service to God our Father.*

As we come to celebrate the Lord's Supper, we are powerfully reminded of Jesus' completed, cleansing work on our behalf. We are reminded of the restored fellowship with God that His shed blood purchased for us. We experience assurance of Christ's constant intercession for us today. And we are also reminded and encouraged by the joyous promise of the hope of our resurrection by faith in Him. Yet we must also partake of the Supper as those called to serve the living God. As those redeemed and regenerated in Jesus, we have received the call to serve. We are first and foremost servants of Christ. But we are also servants to one another for the edification of all the saints in the body. And it is only with the help of the Holy Spirit that we will fulfill this essential call of God upon our lives — *to have this mind among ourselves, which is ours in Christ Jesus... taking the form of a servant* (Philippians 2:5, 7b).

> **PRAYER:**
> Lord Jesus Christ, You came and You lived a sinless life and yet died a sinner's death in order to serve us as our eternal Savior. We offer You all our worship, our praise, and our adoration, for You are the promised Messiah, the Son of the blessed living God. We thank You that through the Spirit's work in us we have been cleansed from the deadness of our former way of living and have been called by You to kingdom service. As we come now to the Supper, Holy Spirit help us to die more fully to ourselves and to live more fully — more abundantly unto Christ our Redeemer and King. In Jesus' name we pray. Amen.

92. Faith, Righteousness, and the Supper

> *And without faith it is impossible to please him, for whoever would draw near to God must believe that he exists and that he rewards those who seek him. By faith Noah, being warned by God concerning events as yet unseen, in reverent fear constructed an ark for the saving of his household. By this he condemned the world and became an heir of the righteousness that comes by faith.*
>
> Hebrews 11:6–7

PRINCIPLE:
The biblical account of Noah in Genesis chapters 6–9 is a most profound example of saving faith in God. The Lord spoke to Noah and revealed to him that He was about to judge the earth for the wickedness of mankind by sending a great flood of waters. Noah was instructed to construct an ark of gigantic proportions and use it to preserve the lives of his immediate family along with suitable pairs of every land animal and bird. In the midst of God's righteous and fierce judgment for sin, He preserved a remnant by means of one faithful man.

We are all familiar with the story, but do we consider the fact that Noah had already lived 600 years upon the earth when the flood came to judge the earth? As set and comfortable as we often get in our ways after 20, or 30, or even 60 years, imagine how used to things in this world we would be after 600 years! And what an unusual task God gave to His servant Noah. Yet, the Bible declares that Noah *in reverent fear constructed an ark*, even though the events about which he had been warned were as yet unseen. By faith, Hebrews explains, Noah *condemned the world and became an heir of righteousness*.

Noah, like Abraham, believed in God, and God declared him to be *righteous before me in this generation* (Genesis 7:1b). It was faith, the Lord's gift to Noah, that enabled him to please God, save his household, condemn sin in the world, and become an heir of the righteousness that comes by faith.

It is this same God-given faith — a faith centered on Jesus Christ — that enables us to please God. It is this same faith that allows us to daily draw near to God in praise and in weekly worship and celebration of the Lord's Supper. It is by this same faith that we became heirs with Noah of the true righteousness purchased by the shed blood of Christ. As we gather around the Lord's Table, let us be reminded that along with Noah and all those commended by God, we share together in the gift of faith and the inheritance of righteousness.

We are the household of faith, saved from the wrath of God's judgment by belief in Jesus Christ. And it is to Christ Jesus' merciful table that we now come.

> **PRAYER:**
>
> Holy Father, we praise You and the Lord Jesus Christ for spreading this merciful Communion table before us. It is truly a gift from You to us with tokens of Christ's body and blood. We cannot adequately express our thanksgiving and our amazement that You have given us faith that, with Noah and Abraham and Jacob, we too are heirs of Your righteousness. We thank You that all of this is placed before our eyes in the bread and the cup of the Lord's Supper. Thanks be to Jesus Christ, Who instructed us to keep this Gospel Feast and Who has spread this merciful table before us. In Jesus' name we pray. Amen.

93. The Heavenly Assembly and the Supper

> *But you have come to Mount Zion and to the city of the living God, the heavenly Jerusalem, and to the innumerable angels in festal gathering, and to the assembly of the firstborn who are enrolled in heaven, and to God, the judge of all, and to the spirits of the righteous made perfect, and to Jesus, the mediator of a new covenant, and to the sprinkled blood that speaks a better word than the blood of Abel.*
> Hebrews 12:22–24

PRINCIPLE:
The author of Hebrews assures us in this passage that as believers in Jesus we have for all intents and purposes really and truly joined ourselves by living faith to the *assembly of the firstborn who are enrolled in heaven*. Our faith in Christ assures us direct access — even to God Himself, *the judge of all*. The soaring, lofty language used in this passage serves to emphasize not only the grandeur and glory of the heavenly realms but our own participation in them as heirs of the new covenant in Jesus. We are not mere spectators you see, but are full participants in the praise and worship of God. The text begins, *But you have come...*, revealing that here is some sense in which this is an ever-present reality for us. It is not only something that sustains our hope for the future, for in worship we enjoy its foretaste in the here and the now.

And what are we to make of the comparison of Abel's blood with Christ's? Remember that the author of Hebrews declares in the previous chapter (11) that, *By faith Abel offered to God a more acceptable sacrifice than Cain, through which he was commended as righteous, God commending him by accepting his gifts. And through his faith, though he died, he still speaks.* This reference to Genesis 4:10, in which God tells Cain, *the voice of your brother's blood is crying to me from the ground*, is used by the inspired writer of Hebrews to emphasize the power and testimony of faith, in this case sealed by martyrdom.

And yet Hebrews declares that while the shed blood of Abel testified to faith and righteousness, the blood of Jesus speaks of the *fulfillment* of faith and righteousness. Abel's blood testifies to the way of faith, but Jesus' blood is the *source and seal* of all true faith. And it is only by the sprinkled blood of Jesus Christ that the faithful are granted the joy and privilege of participation in the heavenly assembly.

John Calvin viewed each celebration of the Lord's Supper as a gathering of God's people upon the earth, who are in effect brought by the Holy Spirit into *the festal gathering and to the assembly of the firstborn enrolled in heaven*. We celebrate together at Communion a prefigurement of the marriage supper of the Lamb, and we are admitted to our places around our Father's Table by the sprinkled blood of Jesus Christ *the mediator of a new covenant*. Our participation in the Sacrament is spiritually linked with the celebration of Communion in Christ enjoyed by *the spirits of the righteous made perfect*, as they gather around God's throne.

> **PRAYER:**
> Lord Jesus Christ, we honor and adore You, we praise and worship You as we come to the bread and the cup of our Communion celebration. We thank You that as we gather around Your Table we are spiritually communing with the righteous who have been made perfect worshiping You in the heavenly places. We praise You that Your have purchased our salvation and adopted us into the Father's family, which is composed of redeemed men, women, and children from every tribe and nation and language and people. We give You praise and honor that this meal is but a small foretaste of the fellowship we will enjoy with You and with all the saints in the heights of glory. May Your name forever be exalted and praised. In Your saving name we pray. Amen.

94. Blessed Is He Who Remains Steadfast

Let the lowly brother boast in his exaltation, and the rich in his humiliation, because like a flower of the grass he will pass away. For the sun rises with its scorching heat and withers the grass; its flower falls, and its beauty perishes. So also will the rich man fade away in the midst of his pursuits. Blessed is the man who remains steadfast under trial, for when he has stood the test he will receive the crown of life, which God has promised to those who love him.

JAMES 1:9–12

PRINCIPLE:
The Apostle James writes some hard things for us to consider as believers in Christ. In this portion of his inspired letter, James reminds us of the temporary and passing nature of wealth and the things of this world — things that so easily distract us from the eternal treasures which are ours through faith in Christ Jesus.

He also reminds us that the Christian life is often fraught with trials and tribulations. Yet again, however, for the Apostle this life remains but a precursor to the eternal life which awaits us afterwards. This pending eternity, marked by our receipt of the crown of life, is what must ever and always shape our view of present riches or present poverty, present blessings or present trials.

Whatever our situations may be today as we come professing faith in Jesus to the Lord's Supper, know that if our hope and confidence is truly centered in Christ alone, we have the free gift of eternal life at work in us today and awaiting us in its fullness in the life which will come after this. Trials and tribulations may indeed come. Many of us may already in fact today be suffering some sort of poverty or affliction. Yet in Christ, all God's riches are stored up for us unto all eternity.

Partaking of the Lord's Supper in genuine God-birthed faith provides His covenant people with sustaining graces through the working of His Holy Spirit. The Sacrament of Communion is a means that God uses to remind us of the crown of life He has promised us in Jesus. It is also a means God uses to strengthen us amidst all the trials and difficulties we face on a regular basis in this present life. The Lord's Supper freshly reminds us that the wealth we may enjoy today, or the poverty we may endure at this time, will be as nothing to us when Christ comes in His full glory, fulfilling His kingdom, and establishing us eternally glorified in His presence.

> **PRAYER:**
> Heavenly Father, please help us to have an eternal perspective concerning the things which we face in this life. May Your Spirit cause us to see the bigger picture of Your purpose and plan to bring us through this journey of life and into the glories and unfading life of eternity future. Whether we know lack or have more than enough, teach us to view our present lives as but steps along the pathway leading to the fullness of Your eternal kingdom. Remind us of these ultimate and certain things as we celebrate the Lord Jesus Christ in the Supper. Give us hope anew in Your faithful promises to us that even as Christ rose from the dead in victory and walks in resurrection light, so also shall we one day rise from the dead, receive the crown of life, and walk in Your blessings in resurrection glory. In Jesus' name we pray. Amen.

95. The Diversity of the Kingdom and the Supper

And they sang a new song, saying,
"Worthy are you to take the scroll
and to open its seals,
for you were slain, and by your blood
you ransomed people for God
from every tribe and language and people and nation,
and you have made them a kingdom
and priests to our God
and they shall reign on the earth."

REVELATION 5:9–10

PRINCIPLE:
When we hear the word *diversity* used today we often associate it with modern cultural attempts to approve of all manner of ideas, lifestyles, religions, and worldviews, without reference to the guiding, defining truth of the Word of God. And yet the term *diversity* is an appropriate one to use in describing what we find in Revelation chapter 5, as the Apostle John reveals the vision he received of the redeemed saints — those whom Jesus has made into a kingdom and priests to God.

The kingdom of Jesus Christ is composed of people *from every tribe and language and people and nation*. The shed blood of God's own Son, the true Passover Lamb, has been applied by God's electing grace through the working of the Holy Spirit, by faith, to ransom a particular people for His own glory. The redeemed people of God's kingdom are composed of the most diverse array of cultures, languages, nationalities, and even periods of time imaginable.

And yet, this diverse array of men, women, and children from every corner of the earth share in one common and binding identity. We are blood-bought covenant children of the living God. We share a common calling as priests to God. And we are all endowed with a magnificent purpose, to reign upon the earth.

It is most appropriate as we gather around the King's Table to ask the Spirit of Christ to remind us of the diversity and immensity of God's ransomed people. Also, that the Holy Spirit will give us a broader sense that we are united by faith around the Table with those who share our identity in Jesus. We dine in the King's presence with them, whatever their language, culture, or nationality. And may we ever be reminded of the shed blood of Jesus Christ, who alone is worthy, and the great work He accomplished on our behalf. For as a result of His glorious mercy and love, displayed in His suffering and death on the cross, we who believe by faith are united in a common calling and purpose — as priests and servants of the King!

> **PRAYER:**
>
> Dear Lord Jesus Christ, we honor You. We adore You. We lift our hearts in praise and thanksgiving before You. Your covenantal kingdom amazes us in so many, many ways. We thank You for purchasing us and all who believe by the blood of the Lamb. We thank You for calling us to be both a kingdom and a royal priesthood. We thank You for tasking us and privileging us to reign upon the earth. We glory in You, King Jesus, our slain and risen Lamb, because You have ransomed us for the Father and for Your glory. Help us now, we pray, to approach this Gospel Feast of the kingdom in awe of You and what You have done for us. Cause us to look upon believers in every place as our family according to God's amazing grace. And by the Spirit encourage us to go forth and fulfill our kingdom calling as priests and vice-regents, bearing the name of Jesus and carrying the banner of our eternal God. In Jesus' name we pray. Amen.

96. Sealed Unto God

After this I saw four angels standing at the four corners of the earth, holding back the four winds of the earth, that no wind might blow on earth or sea or against any tree. Then I saw another angel ascending from the rising of the sun, with the seal of the living God, and he called with a loud voice to the four angels who had been given power to harm earth and sea, saying, "Do not harm the earth or the sea or the trees, until we have sealed the servants of our God on their foreheads."

REVELATION 7:1–3

PRINCIPLE:
The book of Revelation has much to say about the wrath of God poured out upon the earth because of the rejection of God's Messiah, His Son, our Lord and Savior Jesus Christ. And even with the chapters and verses spread out over several weeks of sermons, the theme of divine judgment can be overwhelming and even frightening to those of us who take God's Word as wholly true.

And yet throughout Revelation there is another theme — a theme which like the theme of judgment — reveals the character of God. For just as Yahweh is utterly holy, just, right, and true, so also He is loving, gracious, and compassionate. God describes Himself in Scripture as *slow to anger and abounding in steadfast love.* Just as surely as John's inspired Revelation displays the holiness of God in action and against sin on earth, it also displays the Lord's steadfast and eternal love for those who believe by faith in Jesus Christ.

This passage from Revelation 7 is just one of many passages in the book which teach us and encourage us that if we are in Christ, covered by the blood of the Lamb, we need not fear the wrath of God, or the people, events, trials, and tribulations of this present life. Why? The passage clearly reveals to us that as God's judgment is about to reach its full expression on the earth, God provides protection for His children in Jesus:

Do not harm the earth or the sea or the trees, until we have sealed the servants of our God on their foreheads.

And this revelation of God's loving protection is nearly identical to a passage in the prophet Ezekiel. In Ezekiel's day, God showed to His prophet the departure of His presence from Solomon's temple in Jerusalem. He also showed to Ezekiel the fierce judgment He was going to pour out upon the Jews in Jerusalem. But before a single act of judgment and calamity was allowed to take place, Yahweh instructed His angelic servant to put a mark or seal upon those who longed for the righteousness and true worship of God. Whoever had this mark of belonging to God would be spared and protected (Ezekiel 9).

It is always good for us to remember both the holiness and the love which are central to God's eternal character. For as we more fully understand these two perfect aspects of our Father's character, we also more completely appreciate and appropriate what the Lord has done for us in satisfying both through the saving work of Jesus Christ. Our Savior's work on the cross satisfied God's wrath against our sin and cleansed us of stain and guilt, while at the same time we were declared forgiven and eternally sealed with the mark of God's family and His ever-present love and protection. O, how blessed we are indeed to know God the Father through Jesus Christ His Son!

PRAYER:

Holy and mighty heavenly Father, we praise You that just as You marked Your faithful people in the days of the Exodus using the blood of the Passover lamb; just as You marked Your faithful people in the days of the destruction of Solomon's temple, so You have also marked us and set us apart in Christ Jesus. We thank You that even as You delivered the Hebrews from slavery in Egypt and the believing Jews from destruction in the time of the exile, so also You have saved us from eternal destruction in the fires of hell. How thankful we are, Father, Son, and Holy Spirit, that we are eternally marked — *we belong to Jesus*! As we celebrate the Lord's Supper, help us to embrace this worshipful event as a perpetual symbol of our being set apart in Christ Jesus, our Savior. May the Lord Jesus be ever exalted in our Communion celebration and in every place where the Gospel and the Sacrament are declared among the people of God. In Jesus' name we pray. Amen.

97. Firstfruits for God

> *Then I looked, and behold, on Mount Zion stood the Lamb, and with him 144,000 who had his name and his Father's name written on their foreheads. And I heard a voice from heaven like the roar of many waters and like the sound of loud thunder. The voice I heard was like the sound of harpists playing on their harps, and they were singing a new song before the throne and before the four living creatures and before the elders. No one could learn that song except the 144,000 who had been redeemed from the earth. It is these who have not defiled themselves with women, for they are virgins. It is these who follow the Lamb wherever he goes. These have been redeemed from mankind as firstfruits for God and the Lamb, and in their mouth no lie was found, for they are blameless.*
>
> REVELATION 14:1–5

PRINCIPLE:

In Revelation 14:1–5 we are given yet another glimpse into a heavenly victory celebration. And the way this celebration unfolds reminds us of the various victory songs that precede it in the Holy Scriptures. The episode that immediately comes to mind includes the victory songs of Moses and Miriam in Exodus 15:1–21. The people of God were so overcome with rejoicing for the deliverance God had given them from the oppression and hardship of slavery in Egypt, and they were so amazed at the way that the Lord defeated the mighty chariots of Pharaoh using the Red Sea, that they composed hymns of praise and danced before the Lord.

John sees in this Revelation celebration a group of *144,000 who had [the Lamb's] name and His Father's name written on their foreheads*, and we later learn that these *follow the Lamb wherever He goes* and that *they have been redeemed from mankind*. These redeemed believers are engaged in joyful heavenly worship using a new song that only they could learn. And all the descriptive language John uses about them indicates that they are righteous and they are pure.

Jesus gave this vision to John so that he and the believers in the seven churches in Asia would be encouraged. Our Savior wanted them and He wants us to understand the great blessings we have in the Lamb now and will enjoy alongside these 144,000 one day in the presence of God and the heavenly host. How do we arrive at this application? From the passage, in which Jesus reveals to John that these 144,000 *have been redeemed from mankind as firstfruits for God and the Lamb.* This means that just as the Old Testament celebration of the Feast of Firstfruits represented the expectation of a full harvest to follow, so also this redemptive celebration of God's firstfruits represents the expectation of countless more redeemed men and women to follow.

You and I, if we are believers in Jesus Christ as Lord and Savior, now follow the Lamb in this life and already enjoy the label 'blameless,' for Jesus bore away our sins and gave to us by the Holy Spirit the declaration of His blamelessness. And for this we have every reason to celebrate as well — both in this life and the life that we will enjoy with the Lamb through all eternity. Like the Hebrews of old and these 144,000 of Revelation, we have been delivered from hard bondage — from captivity to sin and the dominion of Satan, into the glorious, eternal kingdom of holiness and grace with God the Father and our risen Lord Jesus as our Head. Just as John's vision uses visual imagery and symbols to declare this great truth, so also does our celebration of the Lord's Supper, as the bread and the cup declare our redemption and justification through our Lamb, Jesus Christ.

PRAYER:
Our gracious and loving heavenly Father, Maker and Sustainer of all things, we praise You for the eternal salvation and the justification of all those who have believed in the name of Jesus Christ. And we praise You that You have set Your redeeming, covenantal love upon us, giving us saving faith and including us in these latter days' harvest of kingdom fruit. Thank You for declaring us righteous because of what Jesus has accomplished as our substitute on that cruel cross. Thank You for visually reminding us every time we receive the Lord's Supper what Jesus has done and how You have transformed us to be conformed after His image. May the Supper continue to be an instrument of Your hand of grace and power at work within us for spiritual renewal, growth, and fruitfulness. In Jesus' name we pray. Amen.

98. Eternal Gospel

> *Then I saw another angel flying directly overhead, with an eternal gospel to proclaim to those who dwell on earth, to every nation and tribe and language and people. And he said with a loud voice, "Fear God and give him glory, because the hour of his judgment has come, and worship him who made heaven and earth, the sea and the springs of water." Another angel, a second, followed, saying, "Fallen, fallen is Babylon the great, she who made all nations drink the wine of the passion of her sexual immorality." And another angel, a third, followed them, saying with a loud voice, "If anyone worships the beast and its image and receives a mark on his forehead or on his hand, he also will drink the wine of God's wrath, poured full strength into the cup of his anger, and he will be tormented with fire and sulfur in the presence of the holy angels and in the presence of the Lamb. And the smoke of their torment goes up forever and ever, and they have no rest, day or night, these worshipers of the beast and its image, and whoever receives the mark of its name." Here is a call for the endurance of the saints, those who keep the commandments of God and their faith in Jesus. And I heard a voice from heaven saying, "Write this: Blessed are the dead who die in the Lord from now on." "Blessed indeed," says the Spirit, "that they may rest from their labors, for their deeds follow them!"*
>
> Revelation 14:6–13

PRINCIPLE:

In this cycle of visions, the Apostle John is presented with an extremely heightened version of the Gospel of Jesus Christ. The emphasis in what the three angels declare is squarely upon the eternal implications and outcomes for those who follow the Lamb on the one hand, and for those who follow the dragon on the other. The consequences for eternity future between believers in Jesus and believers in the ways of fallen mankind could not be made any more clearly or dramatically than they are in this text of Scripture.

We learn that the first angel of the three is sent to declare an eternal Gospel *to every nation and tribe and language and people* — echoing the extent of salvation for those who have been redeemed by the blood of the Lamb in Revelation 5:9. Everyone who dwells on the earth during the time before Jesus' second coming will hear the offer, and the everlasting consequences, of serving the Lord God or serving the devil.

The third angel follows the first two with the dire news of what befalls anyone who serves the beast (representing the devil) instead of following the Lord. This angel reveals that he *will be tormented with fire and sulfur in the presence of the holy angels and in the presence of the Lamb.* Now while we might be tempted to think that this sort of punishment coming as the result of God's wrath for sin would come to an end with the physical death of the wicked, the angel's proclamation makes it clear that this is a never-ending torment. The angel says, *And the smoke of their torment goes up forever and ever, and they have no rest, day or night, these worshipers of the beast and its image, and whoever receives the mark of its name.*

Thanks be to God for His mercy, love and grace in Jesus Christ! Because the direness of eternity for those who reject the Lamb is joined with the sweetness and bliss of those who believe in God's Messiah, the Lord Jesus! The Gospel of eternal salvation is also declared in this passage as another voice from heaven says, *"Write this: Blessed are the dead who die in the Lord from now on." "Blessed indeed," says the Spirit, "that they may rest from their labors, for their deeds follow them!"* This glorious eternal outcome is what awaits those of us who believe in Jesus. And it is the eternal Gospel outcome that is our hope as we gather around the Table for the Lord's Supper, for in it we proclaim the Lord's death — until He returns in glory to usher in the new heaven and new earth and the fullness of the blessings of God upon those He has redeemed. Thanks be to God in Christ!

PRAYER:

Thank You dear heavenly Father, for revealing to us the saving Gospel of our Lord Jesus Christ. Thanks and praise to You and to the Lamb who bring blessing to all those who die believing in You. Thank You for the Sabbath rest which remains for the people of God in King Jesus. We are in awe of Your holiness and righteousness as we approach Your Gospel Feast and remember what Christ has done to save us from eternal damnation. And our hearts long to see everyone come to a knowledge of repentance and redeeming faith in Jesus. As we receive Your great grace in Communion may our desire to see others come to faith be matched by a willingness to be sent to them to share with them the eternal Gospel of Jesus Christ. And it is in His name that we pray. Amen.

99. Until He Comes

> *Then I looked, and behold, a white cloud, and seated on the cloud one like a son of man, with a golden crown on his head, and a sharp sickle in his hand. And another angel came out of the temple, calling with a loud voice to him who sat on the cloud, "Put in your sickle, and reap, for the hour to reap has come, for the harvest of the earth is fully ripe." So he who sat on the cloud swung his sickle across the earth, and the earth was reaped.*
>
> REVELATION 14:14–16

PRINCIPLE:
This passage describes John's vision of the second coming of the Lord Jesus and the final in gathering of the redeemed saints. While the 144,000 earlier in the chapter are described as *the firstfruits for God and for the Lamb*, this later group represents the final peak harvest of the saints in Jesus at His triumphal return. In 1 Thessalonians 4:16–18, the Apostle Paul writes of this same glorious event: *For the Lord himself will descend from heaven with a cry of command, with the voice of an archangel, and with the sound of the trumpet of God. And the dead in Christ will rise first. Then we who are alive, who are left, will be caught up together with them in the clouds to meet the Lord in the air, and so we will always be with the Lord. Therefore encourage one another with these words.*

    The Bible tells us always to be ready for the Lord Jesus' return. Like faithful stewards, given authority over our master's holdings while he is away on a far away business trip, we who serve the Lord Jesus are to always be alert, laboring faithfully, and joyfully anticipating the return of Christ at any moment. When that moment finally arrives, we will see our risen Lord in all His glory and beauty, arrayed just as Daniel saw Him in his vision — just as John also sees Him here, *seated on a cloud like a son of man, with a golden crown on his head*. This is also the fulfillment of the proclamation of the two men who appeared next to the Apostles as Jesus ascended into heaven. The Apostles saw Jesus received by a cloud as He rose out of their sight. At that moment the two men declared to the Apostles that Jesus *will come again in the same way just as you saw him go into heaven.*

    What amazing things will happen the moment of Jesus' triumphant return! All those who have died in the Lord will be raised imperishable — in glorified resurrection bodies like the body of the risen Christ. We who are alive when our Lord returns will also be changed in an instant. And all of us together will accompany Christ in His kingly procession. The new heaven and new earth will be unveiled and those who have rejected Jesus as Lord and Savior will be cast into hell and eternal torment. Yet for those who are in Jesus the second coming of Christ ushers in an eternity of joyfulness, peacefulness, and perfect blessedness in the presence of God and the Lamb.

Each and every time we celebrate the Lord's Supper, the Scriptures tell us that we *proclaim the Lord's death until He comes.* And so as we are reminded by the Holy Spirit of what Jesus did when He died for us upon that cross so long ago, we are also mindful of the blessed hope we share together in the Lord's victorious return. May the Holy Spirit renew your joyfulness and expectation of the return of Jesus as you engage with this Revelation passage and as you share together as covenant brothers and sisters in the Sacrament of the Lord's Supper.

PRAYER:

Heavenly Father, we praise You for the blessed hope — that is, the return of Jesus Christ in glory to judge both the living and the dead. We praise You for delivering us from certain judgment and engrafting us into the family of God. We praise You that we need not fear the coming of King Jesus, but instead look forward to His appearing more and more with each passing day. Holy Spirit, renew our hope in Jesus and increase our joyful anticipation of His return as we come to the Lord's Supper. As we take of the bread representing Jesus' body and as we drink from the cup representing His precious shed blood, may we yearn even more for the fullness of the person of Jesus immediately with us for all eternity. We ask this in Jesus' name. Amen.

100. A Wrath Only Satisfied by Christ

> *After this I looked, and the sanctuary of the tent of witness in heaven was opened, and out of the sanctuary came the seven angels with the seven plagues, clothed in pure, bright linen, with golden sashes around their chests. And one of the four living creatures gave to the seven angels seven golden bowls full of the wrath of God who lives forever and ever, and the sanctuary was filled with smoke from the glory of God and from his power, and no one could enter the sanctuary until the seven plagues of the seven angels were finished.*
>
> REVELATION 15:5–8

PRINCIPLE:
In Revelation 15, John's vision begins to focus upon a great outpouring of the wrath of God upon the rebellious people who have rejected Christ and instead served the dragon. While the first four verses declare the great joy of the redeemed in their praise of God's works of redemption and power, the second four verses introduce the seven bowls of God's wrath, which are fully revealed in chapter 16.

I believe that this portion of Revelation clearly communicates that although God is perfectly merciful and gracious, providing in fact His one and only Son in order to justify His chosen and adopted sons and daughters, He is also perfectly holy and righteous. Therefore, if a sinful man or woman is not a believer in the substitutionary saving work of Jesus, he or she remains subject to the eternal wrath of God against their sin and the sin they inherited from Adam their representative. This is the focus in the second half of chapter 15 and continues into the next chapter.

So what do we learn from this awesome and terrible wrath of God against sin? Well, as believers in Jesus, we should not boast so much in our own salvation and deliverance from eternal judgment. We are permitted to boast in Jesus and the Gospel He has declared. However, we should take away from our encounter with this passage just how fierce the wrath of God is when His perfect holiness confronts our sin. It was this fierce, eternal wrath for our sin that Jesus bore in our place upon that cross so long ago. It has often been said that we really cannot appreciate the price Jesus paid or the suffering He endured on that day on Calvary outside Jerusalem until we understand the depths of our sin and the perfect holiness of God's wrath on account of it.

Secondly, as believers in Jesus we should have a great deal of compassion and concern for all other men and women who live on the earth in our generation, but who have not yet received Jesus as Lord and Savior and thus face the perfect and righteous wrath of God — not only through consequences in this life, but also eternal damnation and torment in the pit of Hell. Instead of arrogance and conceit, we who have received the free gift of salvation in Christ should be the messengers of Jesus' substitutionary suffering and the promise of eternal life through faith in Him.

May the Holy Spirit move and work within us as we gather together around the Lord's Table, enabling us to reflect on just how great a salvation we have received from so great and perfect an act of suffering and love that Jesus has accomplished on our behalf. May we see together how rich the grace of God is in satisfying His own holiness and wrath against our sin through the one-time sacrifice of His only Son. May our hearts be filled with thanksgiving and praise to God for His mercy poured out upon us. And finally, may we moved by the Spirit to make the offer of the Gospel of Christ plain for those who continue to live under the threat of the eternal wrath and judgment of God.

PRAYER:

Our Gracious and loving heavenly Father, we are amazed that although Your holy and just wrath burned hot against us because of our sins, You sent Your one and only Son Jesus Christ to bear all of the pain and anguish of that wrath in our place. And yet, holy Father, when we consider the severity and the eternality of that righteous wrath against sin, we are burdened for all those who have not yet believed in the sweet name of Jesus. And so we now pray, eternal Father, that You will empower us to share the Gospel of King Jesus for saving sinners with everyone who needs to hear it. And we ask You, by Your Holy Spirit, to give them saving faith in Jesus Christ. As we now prepare to go — to be sent by You — may we receive from Your Communion table much fortifying grace and strengthened faith, that we may work in fulfilling Your Great Commission to reach the nations for King Jesus. In Jesus' name. Amen.

101. King of Kings

They will make war on the Lamb, and the Lamb will conquer them, for he is Lord of lords and King of kings, and those with him are called and chosen and faithful.
                                                              REVELATION 17:14

PRINCIPLE:
Despite all of the rebellion against the Lord which is highlighted throughout the book of Revelation, the ultimate theme of Jesus' message to the seven churches and to believers of every generation is contained in this triumphant verse. One of the angels who poured out a bowl of God's wrath provides John with clear encouragement as to where all of the rebellion of humanity and the judgment of God is heading. The final outcome is the complete and absolute victory of the Lord Jesus Christ over all His and our enemies. The angel's declaration is of Jesus the Lamb as Lord of lords and King of kings, the possessor of all authority in heaven and on earth (Matthew 28:18).

This declaration is also encouraging in the way that it describes those who have been saved by faith in Jesus. Believers here are declared to be called and chosen and faithful. It is interesting to note these three terms and even the order in which they occur. We recognize the first two from another famous passage of Scripture: *For many are called, but few are chosen* (Matthew 22:14). Those who are identified with the Lamb in this revelation are not only those who have heard the call of Christ to trust in Him. They are also those few who have been chosen in Jesus from before the foundation of the world, have been given the gift of faith by the Holy Spirit, and have truly believed. The passage also says that those who are called and chosen are also faithful. I take this to mean that as Paul also wrote, *he who began a good work in you will bring it to completion at the day of Jesus Christ* (Philippians 1:6). That is, that although believers are not perfectly faithful in this life, often falling far short of God's beautiful glory and holiness, nevertheless, they are sanctified day by day and are ultimately made perfect at Jesus' return or at their believing deaths. Indeed, although not perfect in this life, all who believe are as the term implies, filled with faith.

If you are a believer in Jesus today, trusting in Him fully and completely as your Lord and Savior — the only source of eternal salvation and blessing, then these declarations from Revelation 17:14 about those who follow Jesus also apply today to you. And just as we celebrate the wonder of Christ's redeeming work in our lives through the declaration of His revealed Word, so also we celebrate His regenerating and sanctifying work in our lives as we gather around the Lord's Table. Just as the bread and the cup visually proclaim the Lord's death until He returns, so also Communion serves to remind us of His call that we be faithful, and at the same time provides His grace to help us to fulfill more fully that call. May you find much blessing and encouragement in God's Word today — written, preached, and visually proclaimed.

PRAYER:
Dear Lord Jesus, we praise You that although we often fall short of Your perfection in this life, one day You will complete the good work that You have begun in us. We also praise You that although it often seems as though the powers of darkness are gaining the upper hand in this present world, in the end You will utterly conquer them as the Lamb Who was slain and yet lives forevermore! We hail You as King of kings and Lord of lords — hallelujah! And as we come partake of the bread and the cup, may the certainty of Your ultimate and complete victory be firmly etched in our hearts and our minds. And may this assurance of Your glorious triumph spur us on in this present life. May we truly believe by faith the promise in Your Word that the gates of hell will not prevail against the testimony of Jesus Christ. We make this prayer in the mighty name of Jesus. Amen.

102. The Lamb's Wedding Supper and the Lord's Supper

> *Then I heard what seemed to be the voice of a great multitude, like the roar of many waters and like the sound of mighty peals of thunder, crying out, "Hallelujah! For the Lord our God the Almighty reigns. Let us rejoice and exult and give him the glory, for the marriage of the Lamb has come, and his Bride has made herself ready; it was granted her to clothe herself with fine linen, bright and pure" — for the fine linen is the righteous deeds of the saints. And the angel said to me, "Write this: Blessed are those who are invited to the marriage supper of the Lamb." And he said to me, "These are the true words of God."*
>
> REVELATION 19:6–9

PRINCIPLE:

The Apostle Paul, writing in Ephesians 5:25–33, draws a direct correspondence between the relationship of a man and woman in the covenant of marriage and the relationship of Christ to His Church. Paul describes how *Christ loved the church and gave himself up for her, that he might sanctify her, having cleansed her by the washing of water with the word, so that he might present the church to himself in splendor, without spot or wrinkle or any such thing, that she might be holy and without blemish.*

We know that ever since His triumphal ascension and the pouring out of the Holy Spirit, Christ has been building His Church and sanctifying its members, all in preparation for His glorious return and the full consummation of His kingdom. The book of Revelation describes for us the great celebration that will take place at Christ's return with His resurrected saints. All who have been redeemed in Christ will be on that day completely sanctified and made ready, much as a bride, adorned in fine pure linen, is beautifully adorned on her wedding day. On that joyous day, all the sanctified and glorified saints composing Christ's Bride the Church will gather in fellowship with Christ the Lamb to celebrate the consummation of all things under the headship of the covenant King.

The Lord's Supper we frequently celebrate acts as a reminder and as a forward pointer for our future hope — the return of Jesus Christ and the great marriage supper of the Lamb. We have, with every

Sabbath day participation in the Supper, the privilege of tasting a sweet and satisfying sample of the much fuller and greater Gospel Feast which is to come in the new heaven and new earth. As we partake together in this foretaste of the great feast of the Last Day, let us reflect upon the profound truth Scripture declares that Jesus Christ is our Head, and we as His assembled Church are also in His eyes the most beloved of brides!

> **PRAYER:**
> Heavenly Father, please make us ready as Christ's perfect Bride. Please continue Your sanctifying work in and through us by Your Spirit that we may be perfectly and spotlessly adorned for our Lord Jesus' great return. Even as brides today and their bridesmaids anticipate and prepare themselves for the wedding celebration, may we also eagerly await and earnestly prepare ourselves for the wedding of Christ and His Church and for the marriage supper of the Lamb. We thank and praise You that in Jesus You have invited us to this most blessed of celebrations. And we also thank You that even in this present life, You have ordained for us a regular Sabbath celebration of the Lord's Supper, which lifts our eyes from the trials of this life toward the new heaven and the new earth coming in the clouds with King Jesus. Adorn us, we pray, Lord Jesus, in Your righteousness and the beauty of Your grace. Amen.

103. Kingdom Dominion

Blessed and holy is the one who shares in the first resurrection! Over such the second death has no power, but they will be priests of God and of Christ, and they will reign with him for a thousand years.

REVELATION 20:6

PRINCIPLE:
How truly blessed we really are if we have faith in Christ Jesus. This is what the Apostle John is saying when he says, *Blessed and holy is the one who shares in the first resurrection!* Through the free gift of faith in Jesus and His atoning death on the cross, we participate also in His resurrection. We share in the victory and the benefits which come as a result of Jesus' triumph over sin, hell, Satan, and death. Because of this, John can also joyfully declare that *the second death has no power* over us. This latter part means that through Christ we have been saved from the eternal condemnation death reserved for those who have not trusted in Him.

King Jesus also revealed to John in this vision of the saints that we are *priests of God and of Christ* and that we will reign with Christ. This is a familiar theme in Revelation for it is just as John unveiled in a previous vision from chapter 5: *Worthy are you to take the scroll and to open its seals, for you were slain, and by your blood you ransomed people for God from every tribe and language and people and nation, and you have made them a kingdom and priests to our God, and they shall reign on the earth.* Our ransom has been paid by the shed blood of Christ and we are now citizens of His kingdom and a royal priesthood of believers, following after Jesus, our Head.

Now these great realities of who we are as believers in Jesus Christ, purchased by His precious blood, are not only waiting for us in some future dispensation of God's redemptive ages. These are truly blessings we currently possess in Christ our Savior. The span of a thousand years' reign proclaimed in this chapter represents the dominion and authority of the true, invisible Church, both its members in this life, and its faithful members who have gone on to be with the Lord, in its mission and work between the first appearing of Christ and His future return in glory. We reign with King Jesus and share in His kingdom authority and in the building of His kingdom through the power of His

Word and by His Holy Spirit. This is the dominion we possess and the calling we have as His kingdom priests and His kingdom agents.

As we come again to the King's table for our Communion celebration, let us do so with the revelation of God's decree that you and I have been saved through faith in Jesus Christ. We come to His Supper in order to be reminded of what He has done for us and to be reminded of who He has redeemed us to be — a kingdom and priests to our God — empowered by the Spirit to exercise kingdom dominion at Jesus' side, following and exercising authority as He leads, guides, and directs. The Lord's Supper is a kingdom feast. It is the remembrance of how Jesus purchased His kingdom and His people. It is the reminder of His kingdom in the present and the work He has for us to do today. And it is the refresher and rekindler of our hope in the return of King Jesus, when the kingdom with reach its fullness, and every knee will bow and every tongue confess Jesus as Lord.

PRAYER:
Heavenly Father, we praise You and thank You that in Christ Jesus You have made us Your priests to the nations and that we will reign on the earth, sitting beside the Lord Jesus on His high and lofty throne. We praise and thank You that the eternal death reserved for condemned has no power over us in Jesus' mighty name! We ask the Holy Spirit to draw us now to this Communion as a sweet foretaste of what Your kingdom will be like at Jesus' return and for all of eternity to come. May we also see Jesus as our continual and great High Priest. And may we also understand more fully what it means that by faith we are now part of the royal priesthood of all believers. In Jesus' name we pray. Amen.

104. You Are Invited

> *Then I saw a new heaven and a new earth, for the first heaven and the first earth had passed away, and the sea was no more. And I saw the holy city, new Jerusalem, coming down out of heaven from God, prepared as a bride adorned for her husband. And I heard a loud voice from the throne saying, "Behold, the dwelling place of God is with man. He will dwell with them, and they will be his people, and God himself will be with them as their God. He will wipe away every tear from their eyes, and death shall be no more, neither shall there be mourning, nor crying, nor pain anymore, for the former things have passed away."*
>
> Revelation 21:1–4

PRINCIPLE:

The Apostle John receives the glorious unveiling of the recreation of heaven and earth in the final two chapters of Revelation. Everything that has taken place in redemptive history from the fall of Genesis 3:1–19 and the Lord's promise to reverse the curse, through the great covenants of God, through the patriarchs, kings, and prophets, up to the appearing of Jesus Christ — then forward through the centuries of the growth of Christ's church — all of it culminates in the full consummation of the restoration of Eden, free of sin, pain, sorrow, and death.

How encouraging this incredible revelation from Jesus must have been to His servant and disciple John! And how encouraging these words must have been to the believers in those seven churches in Asia Minor so long ago. Surely this vision of the return of Christ and the glorification of His saints through eternity must have sustained and given hope to every generation of believers from the time of John to the modern era. And these verses remain just as powerful and glorious for us when we gather as God's people for worship in the 21st century.

Of all the blessings described in this portion of the Revelation, none is more full of promise and encouragement than this: *Behold, the dwelling place of God is with man. He will dwell with them, and they will be his people, and God himself will be with them as their God.* While it is certainly true in the here and now that God is with us, by means of His Holy Spirit, and that He is our God and we are His people, the lofty language and repetition of "with" indicates that God's presence will be fully living and radiating among us on the Last Day.

This simply means that we will know God more fully than we do today and enjoy a much fuller measure of His presence than we do today. God and Christ His Son will truly live and walk alongside us through all eternity future. We will behold God our Father and Jesus our Savior face to face!

This most beautiful promise Jesus makes to us through John in Revelation 21 is actually symbolized for us each time we celebrate the Lord's Supper. Our Lord told His disciples, as He was about to enjoy His Last Supper with them in Luke 22:15–16: *I have earnestly desired to eat this Passover with you before I suffer. For I tell you I will not eat it until it is fulfilled in the kingdom of God.* Jesus on the same night later says to the disciples, *You are those who have stayed with me in my trials, and I assign to you, as my Father assigned to me, a kingdom, that you may eat and drink at my table in my kingdom and sit on thrones judging the twelve tribes of Israel.* So we see that celebrating the Lord's Supper as Christ directed us to do points us symbolically forward to the great marriage supper of the Lamb which we will celebrate when Jesus returns. And the celebration of that future feast at Jesus' return will mark the beginning of our enjoyment of the immediate presence of God the Father and Jesus the Son through all eternity future.

PRAYER:
Lord Jesus, how we long for Your return to us and the celebration of the marriage supper of the Lamb! We thank You for the assurance we have from You and from our heavenly Father that when the appointed time comes, You will descend from heaven with a cry of command, with the voice of an archangel, and with the sound of the trumpet of God. At that hour, the dead in Christ will arise to resurrection glory and we will fellowship with You for all eternity future. We praise You that we will no longer suffer any sorrow or pain and that our joy in You will be complete.

By Your Spirit, help us now to see these future joys with eyes of faith fixed upon You as we gather around the Communion table together. May You receive all of the power, the honor, the glory, and the praise! In Jesus' name. Amen.

SCRIPTURE INDEX

OLD TESTAMENT

Genesis
2:9 3
3:8–9 5
3:1–19 211
3:22 3
4:3–7 7
4:4b–5, 8–9 9
4:10 189
6–9 187
7:1b 187
9:25–27 11
12:1–3 13
14:17–20 15
15:5–6 13
16:13–14 17
17:15–16 19
18:22–23, 25b–26 21
19:23–29 21
22:1–2 23
22:13 23
25:30–34 25
27:22–25 25
28:1–2 27
32:24–30 29
33:4–11 31
41:37–45 67
41:38–41 33

Exodus
12:11–14 35
13:7–20 37
15:1–21 197
15:13, 17–18 39
16:4, 31–32 41
16:12 113
19:6 39
24 x
24:8–11 43

Leviticus
16:15, 17 45
16:20–22 47
17:11 .... 7, 49

Numbers
6:25–26 116
14:17–19 51

Joshua
1:5b–9 53
8:30–31 55

Psalms
2:10–13 57
23:5–6 59
34:8–10 61
81:10 63
84:11–12 65
86:15–17 67
95 57
139:12–14 111

Isaiah
6:1–7 69
7:14 .... 19, 71
9:6–7 73
53:3–6 75
53:6 24
53:10–12 77

Jeremiah
31:31–34 79

Ezekiel
9 196
37:11–14 81
37:23 83

Daniel
7:13–14 85

Habakkuk
3:17–19 87

NEW TESTAMENT

Matthew
- 21:1–11 91
- 22:14 205
- 25:31–40 93
- 26:39ff 125
- 28:1–10 95
- 28:18 205
- 28:18–20 97
- 28:20 98

Mark
- 1:15 99
- 14:24–25 99

Luke
- 1:26–38 71
- 1:50–55 101
- 2:27–32 103
- 15:18–24 105
- 22:14–16 99
- 22:15–16 212
- 22:19 .... ix, 37, 169
- 22:20 .... 13, 125
- 24:25–26 107
- 24:28–32 107

John
- 1:1–2, 14, 16–18 109
- 1:29b 75, 109
- 3:16 111
- 6:25–35 113
- 6:51 41–42
- 6:54 117
- 8:12 115
- 10:14 59
- 10:36 59
- 11:25–26 117
- 13:12–16 119
- 16:13–15 121
- 17 123
- 17:20–23 123
- 18:11 125

Acts
- 1:7–11 127
- 1:8 121
- 2:42 131
- 2:37–41 129
- 20:7 131

Romans
- 1:1–6 133
- 1:16–17 135
- 2:28–29 137
- 3:20 139
- 3:21–22 139
- 3:23 49
- 4:1–8 141
- 4:22–25 143
- 5:1–11 145
- 5:15–17 147
- 6:9–14 149
- 7:21–25 151
- 8:23–25 153
- 8:31–34 155
- 8:31–39 157
- 8:35–39 159
- 12:1 161
- 12:4–8 163
- 12:18 31

1 Corinthians
- 6:13b–20 165
- 7:39b 27
- 11 .... ix, xi
- 11:23–26 .... 10, 167
- 11:24–25 .... ix, 169
- 11:25 14
- 11:26 .... ix, 97, 121, 169, 182
- 11:28 150

2 Corinthians
- 9:6–15 171

Ephesians
- 2:4–7 173
- 2:8–9 26
- 4:5–6 176
- 4:7–8, 11–16 175
- 5:1–2 177
- 5:22–27 27
- 5:25–33 207

Philippians
- 1:6 205
- 2:3–8 120
- 2:5–10 179
- 2:5, 7b 186
- 2:6–7 101

Colossians
- 1:16 109

1 Thessalonians
- 4:16–18 201
- 4:17 59

Hebrews
- 1:1–4 181
- 4:8–10 183
- 9:13–14 185
- 9:22 49
- 9:25–26 45
- 10:4 49
- 10:12 49
- 11:4 7
- 11:6–7 187
- 12:17–24 43
- 12:22–24 189
- 12:28–29 161

James
- 1:9–12 191

1 John
- 3:12 9
- 4:11 10

Revelation
- 5:9 199
- 5:9–10 .... 11, 83, 85, 103, 193
- 7:1–3 195
- 14:1–5 197
- 14:6–13 199
- 14:14–16 201
- 15:5–8 203
- 17:14 205
- 19:6–9 .... 28, 170, 207
- 20:6 209
- 21:1–4 211
- 22 3

www.ingramcontent.com/pod-product-compliance
Lightning Source LLC
Chambersburg PA
CBHW061758110426
42742CB00012BB/1950